THE
ULTIMATE
GUIDE TO
REVERSE
MORTGAGES

ADVANCE PRAISE

This is a FANTASTIC educational resource that hits the right balance of empathy and expertise. I think it could become the go-to book for anyone curious about reverse mortgages — whether they're seniors, adult children, or even financial advisors.

—Dale Corpus, Broker Associate / Realtor, CIAS, CDPE Licensed RCFE Administrator and former mortgage banker

All About Reverse Mortgages breaks down the baffling world of reverse mortgages into clear, simple steps. Casey Fleming provides you with the information you need to consider whether a reverse mortgage makes sense for your financial goals, then tells you how to shop for and get a reverse mortgage. The book is concise and straight-forward, and you don't get bogged down with unnecessary information just to fill up space. This should be required reading for every older American - and their children.

—Kate Horrell, Accredited Financial Counselor, Military Qualified Financial Planner, Owner of Kings High Media at https://KateHorrell.com

I have many elderly, retired clients who own valuable homes but need to preserve their life savings given they have little to no income. The reverse mortgage details and information in Casey's book has been invaluable to me and my clients. I am honored to have worked with Casey on obtaining a much-needed reverse mortgage for my client. Without the information in Casey's book, I was reluctant to move forward; the book is excellent and easy to comprehend from a layman's standpoint.

—Cindy L. Press, CLPF, National Certified Guardian/Certified Paralegal

FINANCING RETIREMENT IN THE 21ST CENTURY

THE
ULTIMATE
GUIDE TO
REVERSE
MORTGAGES

How to Make Them Work for You

CASEY FLEMING

The Ultimate Guide to Reverse Mortgages

How to Make Them Work for You

© 2025 Casey Fleming

Published in San Carlos, California, by Casey Fleming

ISBN 979-8-9930821-0-3 Paperback

ISBN 979-8-9930821-2-7 EPUB

ISBN 979-8-9930821-1-0 Kindle

Cover and Interior Design by:

Ian Koviak

Edited by:

Teresa Mears

This book is dedicated to my wife, Julia, who has taught me that we can maintain a youthful outlook on life while gracefully adding on the years. Since my reverse mortgage clients are, by definition, seniors, this has been a great teaching for me. We boomers have a lot of life left in us, and if we so choose, we can live life to the fullest as long as we're here.

TABLE OF CONTENTS

Introduction. 1

CHAPTER 1 Reverse Mortgage Fact or Fiction 7

CHAPTER 2 The Basics 11

Chapter 3 What Is a Reverse Mortgage? 13

    Product Options 15

CHAPTER 4 The Language of Reverse Mortgages 23

CHAPTER 5 How Much Can You Get? 29

CHAPTER 6 What Can You Do With the Cash? 36

    Purchase a Home. 36

    Pay bills 38

    Enjoy life 38

    Buy Something You've Been Denying Yourself. 39

    Emergencies. 40

    Investment and Cash Management Tool 42

    Retire Early. 42

    Delay Taking Social Security 43

    Home Health Care 43

CHAPTER 7 Qualifying. 45

CHAPTER 8 Costs. 52

CHAPTER 9 What to Expect from the Process. 69

CHAPTER 10 What You Worry About. 77

    Will You Lose the House?. 77

    Can Your Kids Inherit Your Home?. 81

    How Long Can I Live in Our Home if My Spouse Dies? . . 82

    Can They Take Your Home and Kick You Out? 82

CHAPTER 11 Case Studies 83

CHAPTER 12 Risks and Downsides. 90

CHAPTER 13 When to Say "No" to a Reverse Mortgage . . . 92

CHAPTER 14 Alternatives to a Reverse Mortgage 97

About the Author. 102

Glossary. 104

End Notes 108

INTRODUCTION

WHO WANTS TO START a book about possibilities with a bunch of grim statistics? Since you picked up this book—or it was given to you—you probably already know that for most folks, the retirement picture in America doesn't look good.

We still need to talk about the challenges, however, before we talk about a solution. This book will help you decide if getting a reverse mortgage is the best course of action for **you**, given your unique circumstances, goals and concerns.

So, why do people get reverse mortgages? In my experience, clients are trying to achieve one (or more) of four goals: to turn equity into cash when they have limited options, to enhance their quality of life, to handle emergency needs, or as a financial planning tool. Let's take a closer look.

CASH FLOW: THE WAKE-UP CALL

America has a retirement funding problem. We baby boomers—as a rule—did not manage our finances as conservatively as our parents did. A 2024 report from the National Institute on Retirement Security said:

- "When asked if the nation faces a retirement crisis, 79% of Americans agree there indeed is a retirement crisis, up from 67% in 2020."
- "More than half of Americans (55%) are concerned that they cannot achieve financial security in retirement."

According to the Population Reference Bureau, the number of Americans over 65 is expected to double from about 46 million today to more than 98 million by 2060 comprising 24 percent of the U.S. population. The problem of supporting an aging population is not going away.

The bottom line is that most senior Americans have too little saved up for retirement, still have mortgage debt, have difficulty securing a job that pays what they are used to making, and earn too little from Social Security to pay their living expenses.

There is a bright side, however. American homeowners have more equity in their homes than ever before. According to Realtor.com, the total value of owner-occupied homes in the United States reached $48.1 trillion (with a "t") at the end of 2024, with home equity—the difference between the value and mortgage debt—at $34.7 trillion. This means the average home has a mortgage of about 28% of its value. Obviously, some are owned free and clear, and some folks owe much more than 28% of value. While we, as a nation, are woefully short on retirement funding, we have a huge untapped asset—the equity in our homes.

However, qualifying for a conventional mortgage to tap that equity can be difficult, if not impossible, when your income declines dramatically in retirement.

The rules for conventional loans (we'll call them *forward mortgages* in this book) dictate that a lender is required to document that you have the ability to make the payments on the proposed loan for the anticipated life of the loan. Your gross income must be high enough to cover all of your monthly expenses, including mortgage, property tax, insurance and other property-related expenses, plus any other debt you might have, such as credit cards, car loans, etc., **plus** enough of a cushion for living expenses. In other words, to qualify for a conventional loan you should have enough income that you don't need to draw from savings in order to pay your bills.

But, in retirement, that's exactly what we do. We are done working for a living, we have a little income coming in, and we've saved up some money (hopefully). We've reached the *draw-down* phase of our lives, as financial planners like to call it. If we are fortunate, we are enjoying the good life -- resting on our laurels, so to speak. This is the time of life when we are *supposed* to be spending our children's inheritance.

So, most folks simply can't qualify for a forward mortgage after retirement. If your payments are too high and you are living hand-to-mouth, your only options are to tough it out, sell your home, or consider a reverse mortgage.

You, however, are not a statistic. You are a real person, with a real home, and challenges you are trying to solve or goals you want to achieve. So, let's talk about *you*.

QUALITY OF LIFE: IT'S TIME TO PLAY

Not everyone gets a reverse mortgage because it's their only option. Some folks consider reverse mortgages because they are healthy, vibrant and active and they want to travel, explore, do all the things they always wanted to do but never had the time. Many, however, now have the time, but not the money. They do have equity, though -- equity they can't touch, because they can't qualify for a forward mortgage, or even a conventional equity line.

For these folks, accessing their equity via a reverse mortgage is not about solving some dire financial challenge in their lives—it's about living their lives to the fullest, using the hard-earned equity they've built in their biggest asset, their home.

COVERING EMERGENCIES

Anyone who lives on a fixed income and has very thin savings is only one emergency away from a financial crisis. A car breakdown, a home repair, or the most common issue for seniors, a medical issue, can create a crisis that can't be overcome. The typical fixed income that seniors have is too little to recover financially over time, and unless they can go back to work, they have no way to increase their incomes.

This leaves seniors with bankruptcy as the only viable option. According to U.S. News and World Report, the number of seniors in the United States filing bankruptcy was almost five times greater in 2016 than it was in 1991.

Yet, these seniors often have built up equity in their homes, which they can use to pay for emergencies. There are certain structures for reverse mortgages that are very well suited to that exact issue, which we'll be discussing in this book.

FINANCIAL PLANNING TOOL

While some folks believe that reverse mortgages only make sense for the desperate, savvy financial planners are starting to discover something remarkable. They have long advised clients to have an equity line as a financial planning tool. The thought process goes like this: When stock prices are down, it is a terrible time to withdraw money from your investment accounts. It's better to wait until the market goes back up again.

At the time when it is most crucial to maximize long-term returns on savings and investments, seniors often have no choice but to make a financial move that hurts them—unless they have an equity line they can use for expenses until the market comes back.

But in retirement, folks often can't qualify for an equity line. However, *a reverse mortgage can be set up as an equity line.* Many folks with a robust investment portfolio are using reverse mortgages set up as an equity line as an elegant financial planning tool.

WILL IT HELP *YOU*?

It doesn't really matter why others get a reverse mortgage.

The important question is, what can a reverse mortgage do for *you*? Why are *you* interested in learning about reverse mortgages?

The purpose of this book is to dispel myths about reverse mortgages (there are many) and to clearly explain the benefits, costs and risks of the various options and alternatives that you may want to consider. A reverse mortgage is *not* for everyone, and there is no one type of reverse mortgagethat is right for everyone. This book should help you answer three basic questions:

What problem am I trying to solve? (Or, for a more positive outlook, "What benefit am I really looking to achieve?")

Will a reverse mortgage help me achieve my goals? (And, if so, which product is best for my circumstances and concerns?)

What do I give up when I get a reverse mortgage?

NOTES ABOUT THIS BOOK

I'd like to mention a couple of things about this book before we dive in.

First, the information in this book has been developed through the study of reverse mortgage products, of course, but also through the practice of working with clients and writing loans. The factual information about reverse mortgages was drawn from these experiences.

I also teach classes to consumers about reverse mortgages through local community education organizations, through colleges and local school districts. I have learned a great deal from my students by listening to their needs and concerns and discussing them in a group environment. The ideas and opinions about how reverse mortgage products work in real life came as much from my students as from my professional practice and experience.

Second, we are going to have an uncomfortable conversation here and there in this book. A reverse mortgage is meant to be a lifetime product; it is meant to last for your lifetime. Put another way, it is meant to last for as long as you do.

It is impossible to clearly describe how some parts of the reverse mortgage product work without acknowledging that this means lenders think about how long you are going to live. Part of their calculation includes your *expiration date* according to actuarial tables.

I have found in my classes that seniors are, as a rule, very comfortable with this conversation. Their children (who often accompany them to classes) are *decidedly not*. If you have picked this book up because your parents are thinking of getting a reverse mortgage and you want to know more about it, then please be aware—we are going to discuss how long your parents are likely to live.

Finally, if you see a term that is new to you and it is italicized, that will usually mean that the term is defined in the glossary. There are also hyperlinks throughout the book to helpful online resources.

Now, let's have a primer on exactly what a reverse mortgage is, how they are structured, how much you can get and what they cost.

And thank you for picking up this book!

CHAPTER 1

REVERSE MORTGAGE
FACT OR FICTION

THERE ARE SO MANY MYTHS about reverse mortgages. Consumers often decide whether or not to get a reverse mortgage based on misinformation. Let's start this book by examining everything you've heard about reverse mortgages (and maybe some things you haven't heard) to separate fact from fiction.

Getting a reverse mortgage reduces the amount of money your heirs will inherit when you die. Fact. When you get a reverse mortgage, you are spending your children's inheritance, at least some of it—but not as much as you might think. You'll see why later in this book.

When you get a reverse mortgage, the bank owns the house. Fiction. You retain title to the house. Your home will still belong to you. You may sell it at any time, pay off the mortgage, and keep the rest of your money. You can refinance and pay off the reverse mortgage at any time without penalty and still own the house. If you win the lottery, you can pay off the reverse mortgage and own your home free and clear. When you pass away you can leave the house to your heirs. (Any heirs that you choose). They will have to pay off the mortgage, but the home is yours to bequeath as you wish.

A reverse mortgage eats into your home's equity. This is partly true. You do not have to make payments on a reverse mortgage, but there is interest charged every month. That interest is added to the balance of your loan. However, reverse mortgages are very conservative. They will lend you much less than a conventional mortgage would. We're going to do a little math here, so bear with me.

Let's say your home is worth $500,000, and you are in your 70s, so you can get a reverse mortgage of $200,000. Your home is appreciating at, say, 4 percent per year, and the reverse mortgage interest rate is, say, 7 percent per year. The first year your home will appreciate $20,000 ($500,000 x 4 percent) and the reverse mortgage will grow by $14,000 ($200,000 x 7 percent.) Despite the reverse mortgage, you *gained* $6,000 of equity in the first year.

After a few years the mortgage will increase faster than your home appreciates, if these assumptions are true, but that's usually many years from now.

If you are underwater (owe more than your home is worth) they can take your home away from you. Fiction. Your reverse mortgage is a lifetime loan. No matter how long you live, no matter how much you owe, you can live in your home as long as you want.

If you owe more than your home is worth when you die, your heirs have to pay the difference. Fiction. All reverse mortgages today are non-recourse loans, meaning that if you are underwater when you die, your heirs can sign over title to the lender, but neither your estate nor your heirs have to pay any additional money to the lender.

Reverse mortgages are more expensive than conventional mortgages. Fact. A reverse mortgage is more expensive because it is riskier for the lender in a couple of major ways. We just covered one—if you live long enough to be underwater on your home, the lender may lose money.

But there's something else. With a conventional mortgage, the lender knows exactly how and when they're going to get paid back. Moreover, every month they get paid back a little of their principal, so each month the amount of money they have at risk goes down. With a reverse mortgage, the balance of your mortgage increases over time and the lender doesn't know when they'll get paid back. It could be one year, it could be eight, it could be 40. They don't know, and, until that day comes, they have no access to the capital they've lent you or the interest they are earning. They have no idea when they are going to see that money.

If you were a lender and had a choice of investing in either a conventional mortgage or a reverse mortgage at the same interest rate, you would choose to invest in the conventional mortgage every time. But the higher return on a reverse mortgage makes up for the risk so investors are willing to invest a portion of their mortgage-related investments in reverse mortgages, too.

You don't have to qualify to get a reverse mortgage. Fiction. Qualifying is not as difficult as with a conventional mortgage, because you don't need to prove that you have enough income to make payments. However, you still need to have enough income to pay your monthly property expenses (property taxes, insurance, maintenance expenses and HOA dues, if any) and enough equity to qualify for the reverse mortgage. If you don't have enough income to cover your monthly property expenses, the lender can usually set up a fund to pay these for you. (See Chapter 4.)

Your home has to be free and clear to qualify for a reverse mortgage. Fiction. If you have enough equity, you can use a reverse mortgage to pay off your existing mortgage plus generate cash, monthly payments or an equity line. Additionally, there is now a second mortgage reverse product that does not require you to pay off your existing mortgage. (More on this in Chapter 3.)

You can only get a reverse mortgage on your personal residence. Fact. You must live in your home to qualify for a reverse mortgage, and you must continue to live there. If you move out of your home for any reason for longer than 12 months, your reverse mortgage is due and payable.

In the next chapter, you'll get an overview of reverse mortgages. In subsequent chapters you'll find all the nitty-gritty of product types, terms, costs, risks and benefits. If you read only Chapters 1 and 2, you'll still have a good understanding of what reverse mortgages are, and are not, as you go shopping.

CHAPTER 2

THE BASICS

A REVERSE MORTGAGE is one where you do not have to make payments if you don't want to.

Your money comes to you in one of three ways:

- All at once.
- As monthly payments.
- Only when you need or want it.

For a reverse mortgage, all of these things are true.

You still own your home.

You still own any appreciation in your home.

You must live in (or be purchasing) your home.

You must continue living in your home to keep a reverse mortgage.

You must pay your taxes and insurance and maintain your home.

Interest is accruing on your mortgage, so you will owe more over time.

You can make payments if you want to, to reduce the impact interest accrual has on your equity.

If you move out, you can sell the home, pay off the mortgage, and keep the rest of your equity.

If you are ever "underwater," meaning you owe more than

your home is worth, the lender cannot come after you or your estate for the difference.

If you die, your heirs inherit your home, and they can pay off the mortgage in one of three ways:

- Sell the home.
- Refinance it with a conventional loan.
- Pay it off with cash.

That's it. These are the things that define a reverse mortgage, how it works and how it will affect you and your family.

The rest of this book simply dissects all the fine details of reverse mortgages to help you understand what you need to know to decide if you want to move forward and, if so, how best to do so. Here's what we'll cover.

- What is a reverse mortgage?
- What options do you have with a reverse mortgage?
- The language of reverse mortgages—terms you need to know.
- How much money can you get?
- What can you do with the cash?
- How do you qualify for a reverse mortgage?
- How much do reverse mortgages cost?
- How to avoid pitfalls.
- Benefits of a reverse mortgage.
- Risks of a reverse mortgage.
- How to use a reverse mortgage to achieve your goals, if one is right for you.
- Alternatives to a reverse mortgage.

CHAPTER 3

What Is a Reverse Mortgage?

A REVERSE MORTGAGE is Simply the Reverse of a Forward Mortgage.

OK, maybe that's too simple. But the **differences** can be summed up as:

- *When* you get the money you are borrowing.
- Your *obligations.*
- When and how your reverse mortgage gets paid off.
- The *term* of the loan.

Let's take a look.

WHEN WILL YOU GET THE MONEY YOU BORROW?

With a forward (conventional) mortgage, the bank advances you the money all at once. Then, you pay it back a little bit every month for the rest of your life. (So it seems, anyway, as you keep paying for the term of the mortgage, often 30 years.) Simple.

A reverse mortgage works differently. The lender may give you all the money you intend to borrow up front, or it may give you some of the money up front and the rest when you need it, or all the money in monthly payments over time. More importantly, you don't ever have to make payments. (In most cases you can, but you are not required to.)

NO MORTGAGE PAYMENTS

With a forward mortgage, because you are making payments, the principal balance (the amount you owe) declines every month, until you pay it off entirely. At that point, you've paid back all the money you borrowed, plus interest, you owe nothing against your home.

With a reverse mortgage, since you make no payments, the interest being charged *accrues*; the accrued interest is added to the loan balance. The amount you owe on the loan grows larger every month.

WHEN AND HOW IS THE LOAN PAID OFF?

With a forward mortgage, you make payments until the loan is paid off, and then you stop.

With a reverse mortgage, the loan does not come due until you either pass away, sell your home, or stop living in your home as your primary residence (for any reason) for more than 12 months. If any of these things happens, it triggers a *call* for the loan; the loan is due and payable in full. (Although you are given time to review your options and to figure out how you want to pay it back.)

If you stop living in your home, you have several options to pay off the loan:

- You may refinance into a conventional loan, if you qualify. Of course, the new lender will want you to make payments on the new loan.
- You can pay off the loan with cash that you have in savings or investments.
- You can sell the home and use the proceeds to pay off the reverse mortgage, keeping whatever is left over from the sale.

If you pass away in your home, your heirs have the same three options to pay off the reverse mortgage.

The important point here is that although you must pay back the loan, plus interest, the home is still yours and you don't have to make monthly payments.

TERM – WHEN THE LOAN IS PAID OFF

With a forward mortgage the term, or length of the loan, is defined in your contract. If you've ever gotten a forward mortgage, you are familiar with the Note; this is your agreement to repay the loan in a forward mortgage. The most common term for a forward mortgage is 30 years. You borrow the money and pay it back month by month until it is paid in full, in 30 years.

With a reverse mortgage, the term ends when the last borrower passes away, when you sell the home for any reason, or when it is no longer your primary residence for more than 12 months. With a reverse mortgage the term is not defined in years. It is a lifetime loan. As long as you live in the house, you don't have to pay it back.

PRODUCT OPTIONS

There are quite a few ways in which you can receive money with a reverse mortgage, so you'll have some options. Before we jump into the various ways you can receive the money, however, we need to discuss the two different basic categories of reverse mortgages: FHA-insured, and non-FHA-insured.

HECM VS. "JUMBO"

Most reverse mortgages made today are insured by FHA—the Federal Housing Administration—and are known in the industry as *HECM*s. HECM is an acronym for Home Equity Conversion Mortgage. (You are *converting* your home equity into cash.) When you hear lenders talking about it, you'll find they pronounce it "heckum."

WHAT DOES FHA INSURANCE DO?

FHA mortgage insurance protects the lender primarily, but in doing so also protects you—or at least your heirs. If the lender cannot recover the principal that they advanced to you because the home value is lower than what you owe, the lender will not lose money. How?

If the balance on your HECM reaches 95% of the current appraised value, FHA will purchase the loan from the lender. Since lenders have less risk with a HECM because of this insurance, they are willing to accept a lower interest rate than with other similar mortgages.

To be insured by FHA, a reverse mortgage must meet FHA guidelines. These guidelines include:

- The *Maximum Claim Amount* (we'll explain this shortly) can be no greater than the *Conforming Loan Limit* (ditto) for your area.
- If you have a condo, your condominium project must be FHA-approved.
- The home must meet certain guidelines regarding its condition. In general, it must be safe, clean and properly maintained.
- Your income must be sufficient to cover basic expenses.

There are other requirements, but these are the ones that typically come up when writing a HECM.

There is one limitation to HECMs that can affect many homeowners. When they calculate how much you can borrow, lenders use a percentage of what you might think of as the appraised value. However, the maximum value they will use is limited to the current *conforming loan limit* in your county. We'll cover this indepth in Chapter 7, *Qualifying*, but for now figure that if your property is worth more than the average home across the nation, the amount you can borrow might be limited.

Link: What is the current conforming loan limit?

If you need or want more money than a HECM will provide, or if your home does not qualify for FHA mortgage insurance for any reason, then you will have to consider a *proprietary reverse mortgage*, more commonly called a *jumbo reverse mortgage*. Proprietary reverse mortgages tend to have limited options in terms of how they are structured compared to HECMs, but work well when a HECM won't.

Jumbos do tend to be more conservative because the lender isn't insured, and thus has to eat any deficiency if you are underwater when the loan is paid off. The maximum you can borrow, therefore, is less than a HECM if your home is worth less than the current conforming loan limit. However, if the value of your home exceeds the conforming loan limit in your area significantly, you may be able to borrow a great deal more using a proprietary reverse mortgage. We'll explore this later with examples.

What this means to you is that your reverse mortgage will either be a HECM, and thus the lender is insured by FHA mortgage insurance, or it will be a proprietary, or "jumbo," meaning it will not be insured.

Once we've determined whether an FHA-insured HECM or a non-FHA-insured jumbo is best for you, we can take a look at the different ways in which you can receive the money.

LUMP SUM

Also known as the *Single Disbursement Lump Sum*, this option is a good solution if you have a relatively large mortgage and simply want to eliminate payments for the rest of your life. The lender will advance you enough money to pay off your current mortgage and pay for all the costs associated with originating the loan and give you additional cash if you have enough equity.

You will receive no more payments after your loan closes with a lump sum reverse mortgage. This is essentially a "set it and forget it" loan. You will take out the loan, make no payments, and your heirs will pay off the loan plus interest when they inherit the property.

The lump sum loan is also an excellent option for someone who wants to buy a home using a reverse mortgage. That's right; you can use a reverse mortgage to buy a home, if you have a large enough down payment.

For HECM loans, the lump sum reverse mortgage is the only one that has a fixed interest rate. However, rules for the lump sum generally mean that you will be able to access less of your equity than with other types of HECMs.

MONTHLY PAYMENTS

If you do not have a large mortgage currently and want to receive monthly payments to help with cash flow, the *Monthly Tenure* reverse mortgage could be right for you. With this mortgage, you receive an initial disbursement large enough to pay off your existing mortgage plus all closing costs, and then you'll receive monthly payments for the rest of your life, as long as you continue living in your house.

A monthly tenure reverse mortgage always has a variable

interest rate, and, as of this writing, is available only as a HECM. No jumbo lender currently offers this loan.

A variation on the monthly tenure loan is a *Monthly Term Reverse Mortgage*. With the monthly term reverse mortgage, you'll receive payments for a set number of years, rather than for the rest of your life. Since the lender knows how long it will have to make payments and how much to advance in total, the lender can usually offer you more income per month than with a monthly tenure loan.

For a while, jumbo reverse mortgages were available with this feature. As of this writing they are not, but hopefully they will come back.

REVERSE MORTGAGE LINE OF CREDIT

By structuring your reverse mortgage as a *line of credit,* you can receive advances only when you request them. The advantage is that you don't have to pay interest on money you haven't yet drawn, and when you do need funds, you can draw as much as you like, up to the credit limit. An additional advantage is that the amount available to you through the line of credit can grow over time, if you don't use it up.

The *HECM line of credit* is best used if you don't have the need for monthly payments, but occasionally need cash for emergencies or perhaps have large periodic expenses, such as property taxes. It is also very useful if you have a decent investment portfolio but don't want to draw on it when the market is down. You can use the equity line feature to fund your expenses until the market recovers, then sell stocks only after they have recovered their value, using the proceeds to pay off the equity line. Both the HECM and jumbo line of credit options always have variable interest rates.

COMBINATION

Most reverse mortgages are set up as a combination of two of the above options. You receive enough of an initial draw as a lump sum to pay off your existing mortgage plus closing costs and any cash that you need right away, and then receive monthly payments or set up an equity line to draw money when you need it.

The advantage of setting your reverse mortgage up as a combination is that you don't pay interest on the money until you receive it. Should you not need it for a while, your loan balance will grow much more slowly than if you take all the funds at once.

PROPRIETARY, OR "JUMBO" REVERSE MORTGAGES

If you don't qualify for a HECM, you'll want to consider a proprietary, or jumbo, reverse mortgage. Most homeowners who pursue a jumbo do so because the value of their home is high and a HECM will not generate enough cash for them.

Jumbo reverse mortgages are usually set up with a lump sum payout. They are also available as equity lines. There are no lenders today offering jumbo reverse mortgage with the monthly payment option. There is also a new product on the market in the form of a second mortgage. We will dive into that shortly.

The interest rates on jumbo reverse mortgages are higher than on HECMs, because the lender is not insured against loss. However, there is no monthly mortgage insurance, and no up-front mortgage insurance fee. (See Chapter 8, *Costs*.) This feature can save you quite a bit of money.

Because the lender is not insured, lenders will lend a smaller percentage of the value of your home. However, you may still qualify for more money with this product anyway, because the lender is not limited to using the conforming loan limit for the Maximum Claim Amount (the basis to calculate how much cash you can get.) If you recall from earlier in the chapter, HECMs are limited to what they can use as the value for the basis to calculate how much money you can get. Jumbo lenders can use whatever your home is worth. In high-value areas, this usually means you can access more of your equity.

In short, a jumbo reverse mortgage is usually cheaper to set up, but more expensive over time. It offers fewer options as to how you can receive your money, but usually provides you with more cash.

Let's take a look at the newer, more innovative products that have come out recently.

SECOND MORTGAGE

A new reverse mortgage product emerged in 2023 that is structured as a second mortgage. This is the only reverse mortgage product available that allows you to keep your existing first mortgage. Why would you do this?

In 2020 through 2021, mortgage rates dropped to historically low levels. During this time, most homeowners refinanced into an extraordinarily low interest rate on fixed-rate mortgages. Those interest rates are long gone, and most likely will never return, but homeowners with these loans don't want to give up those low rates, even to access equity. The cost of owning their home is insanely low because of the low interest rate. Many are reluctant to give up that low-rate mortgage, even to access equity.

Enter the reverse mortgage second. This product will allow you to access the idle equity in your home without paying off your low-rate first mortgage. You'll still need to make payments on the first mortgage, but that might be just fine for you.

NOTE: This product eats into your equity at a much slower pace than a conventional reverse mortgage. Your second mortgage balance is rising just like any other reverse mortgage as the unpaid interest accrues, but you are still paying down your first mortgage.

The second mortgage reverse is a lump-sum loan. The interest rate on the reverse second mortgage is fixed and, like other reverse mortgages, this mortgage is a lifetime loan. That means you never have to pay it back unless you move out, and you never have to make a payment.

CHAPTER 4

THE LANGUAGE
OF REVERSE MORTGAGES

A REVERSE MORTGAGE is simple in concept but quite complex in practice. Besides needing to sort out the lenders and options that work best for you, you will be buried in terms that you may not have heard before, many of which are unique to reverse mortgages.

Understanding these terms will help you better understand and evaluate what you are being offered. The following terms are the ones that you should know and understand.

MAXIMUM CLAIM AMOUNT

The *maximum claim amount* is the dollar amount that the lender uses to determine how much they want you to owe when you reach your expiration date. (I told you we were going to have this uncomfortable conversation.) When they expect your life to be over, they want you to owe no more than this amount (approximately.)

Think of the maximum claim amount as the equivalent of an appraised value in a conventional mortgage. In fact, for most reverse mortgage borrowers it will be your appraised value. However, if you are getting a HECM loan and the value of your home is higher than the conforming loan limit in your county, your maximum claim amount will be capped at a ceiling. This ceiling is set each year by the *Federal Housing Finance* Agency (FHFA) and is known as the *conforming loan limit*.

To see what this means practically, see Chapter 5, *How Much Can You Get?*

INITIAL PRINCIPAL LIMIT

The Initial Principal Limit is the maximum amount of your equity that you can *receive* from your reverse mortgage. Note that it is lower than the maximum claim amount. The initial principal limit is determined by multiplying the maximum claim amount by the *Principal Limit Factor*. This factor is driven by your age and interest rate. The older you are, the more you can borrow, and the lower your expected interest rate, the more you can borrow.

UNPAID PRINCIPAL BALANCE

The *unpaid principal balance* is the amount you owe on your mortgage at any given point in time. If you make no payments, the unpaid principal balance grows.

INITIAL DISBURSEMENT LIMIT

There is one more refinement to the initial principal limit. The *initial disbursement limit* is the maximum amount you can take in the first year you have your reverse mortgage.

In the past, many seniors took out reverse mortgages and either were persuaded to invest the funds in annuities, or just blew the money on a good time. The FHA decided that seniors were being hurt by this and limited the amount of funds that a borrower can access in the first year to 60% of the initial principal limit.

However, there is an exception. When you get a reverse mortgage, you must pay off your existing mortgage and any other liens against the property (unless you choose a reverse second mortgage), plus any charges for the loan in escrow. Your existing mortgage will be paid off in escrow with the funds the reverse mortgage lender advances to you. What if this exceeds 60% of the initial principal limit?

Then you can take enough out initially to pay off all your liens and pay the costs of getting the mortgage (together these are known as *mandatory costs*), plus a small amount of cash. So, if this is the case, your initial disbursement limit is greater than 60%, but never more than the initial principal limit.

INITIAL RATE

The initial interest rate is the interest rate as defined in your Note, whether fixed or variable. In the case of a fixed-rate loan, it is fixed for the life of the loan. In the case of a variable-rate loan, it is fixed for a defined period of time, and then will adjust, either monthly or annually.

EXPECTED RATE

The *expected rate* is the average interest rate a lender expects you to pay over the course of the loan. For a fixed-rate reverse mortgage, this is, of course, very easy—it's the interest rate defined by your Note.

On adjustable-rate mortgages, it's a little different. The lender knows—and you know—that your interest rate on the Note is only a starting point. But how can anyone predict what your average interest rate will be, when they don't know how long you'll keep the loan or, for that matter, what interest rates will be?

Lenders turn to the smartest minds in the room to divine this answer. Institutional investors who move billions of dollars a day not only invest in buying debt-based securities (like bonds) but they also *bet on where interest rates will go in the future* through different securities and different types of trades.

Investors sometimes swap risk and return with each other. The mechanics of how they work is well beyond the scope of this book (and above my pay grade) but, in short, lenders look at the current yield on certain types of investment bets to determine what investors believe would be a reasonable rate of return over a given time frame. In other words, they predict where variable interest rates will be, on average, over time. To determine the expected rate, investors look at a 10-year period.

These investors are extremely well-educated folks moving billions of dollars a day for a living. Presumably, they know what they are doing. So, your reverse mortgage lender uses this rate to predict where your interest rate is likely to be—the *expected rate*. Note that this isn't guaranteed, just a benchmark that they expect will be the average rate you'll pay over the life of your loan.

The expected rate is important because it is used to determine how much you can borrow. We mentioned in a previous section that the initial principal balance is a function of the maximum claim amount, your age, and the interest rate. But which rate? The rate they use for this calculation is the *expected* rate, not the initial interest rate. So, in times when markets are unstable and investors fear interest rates will rise in the future, your borrowing power will be less.

MANDATORY CHARGES

Mandatory charges are those charges that must be paid at or before closing. They include all liens against your property:

- Mortgages.
- Home equity line of credit.
- Property taxes that are either past due or due within 60 or 90 days (depending on the lender).
- Tax liens.
- Any other lien, voluntary or not.

They also include the costs associated with arranging your mortgage:

- Upfront mortgage insurance premium, if any.
- Counseling fee.
- Appraisal fee.
- Origination charges.
- Lender fees.
- Title fees.
- Escrow fees.
- Recording charges.

You can pay any or all of these charges in cash, or you can finance them into your new reverse mortgage, as long as your initial principal limit is high enough to do so. If you finance them, the total amount of the charges will be deducted from the cash advanced to you in your initial disbursement.

LESA, OR LIFE EXPECTANCY SET-ASIDE

Do you need or want your lender to pay your property taxes and insurance when they come due?

With a conventional mortgage, you may pay the lender a little extra along with your monthly payment to fund an escrow fund, from which the lender pays your property taxes and homeowner's insurance. You don't *have* to have an escrow (also known as an impound) account in most cases, but you may choose to have one anyway, even if it is not required.

With a reverse mortgage you don't make payments. So, there are no payments to fund an escrow, or impound account. Instead, the lender can set up a fund when they make your loan to make the payments for the duration of your life expectancy by setting aside enough money from your initial principal limit. If you set this up, you'll have less money available up front, but your property taxes and insurance will be paid by the lender on your behalf for the rest of your expected life (as determined by actuarial tables). This fund is known as a *life expectancy set-aside*, or LESA. (Pronounced as the woman's name, Lisa.)

A LESA will be *required* if your monthly income is deemed insufficient to cover your basic living expenses, plus taxes and insurance.

In most cases you will not be required to have a LESA, but you may elect to have one anyway.

However, note that the fund is meant to cover these expenses for the duration of your life expectancy. What happens if you outlive the actuarial tables? Your escrow account will be out of funds, and you will have to begin making these payments yourself.

All other terms of the reverse mortgage remain in place, and you still have the right to stay in your home for as long as you live—provided you pay your taxes and insurance on your own after the fund runs out (although you could refinance into another reverse mortgage at that time).

CHAPTER 5

How Much Can You Get?

IN OUR DISCUSSION of terms above we touched on the basics of the *initial principal limit.* Now, let's dive into the mechanics of how it works. First, let's review the factors that go into the calculation.

FACTORS

MAXIMUM CLAIM AMOUNT

The *Maximum Claim Amount* is the first number used to determine how much money you can borrow, in the same way that an appraised value is used to determine your maximum loan amount on a forward mortgage.

The maximum claim amount represents the maximum amount of exposure the lender wants to have *at the time they believe you will likely expire.* This can be confusing, because in most cases the maximum claim amount is the same as the appraised value. In a forward mortgage the maximum the lender wants to lend you is described as the loan-to-value ratio, while in a reverse mortgage the maximum the lender wants to lend you when you first acquire the loan is called the *initial principal limit.*

So, in reverse mortgages we have to think differently, because the language and the terms are very different.

First, let us repeat: In most cases, the maximum claim amount equals the appraised value. This means that there are cases when it doesn't, and that bears explaining.

In our previous chapter we explained that most reverse mortgages are HECMs, and that the rest are commonly called "jumbos." A HECM must meet FHA guidelines, and one of those guidelines is that the **maximum claim amount cannot exceed the conforming loan limit for your county**.

Does this mean that if the value of your home is higher than this number you can't get a HECM loan? No, it means that even if your home appraises for more than that number, the maximum claim amount will be set at the conforming loan limit.

This begs the question: "What is the conforming loan limit for my county?" There is always a national standard, and since 2008 there has been a second standard, too, which applies to high-cost areas. To find the conforming loan limit for your specific county, simply click here, and then open the Loan Limit Lookup Table. (You'll need Excel to see it.) If you have a hard copy of this book, search for "FHFA Confirming Loan Limit by county" on the internet. Click on the link to Fannie Mae, Freddie Mac or the Federal Housing Finance Agency (FHFA.) Ignore all other links; those are companies that want to sell you something.

The important thing to remember is that in the case of a HECM, your maximum claim amount will either be your appraised value or the conforming loan limit in your county, *whichever is less*.

For jumbo loans, the maximum claim amount will be the appraised value, unless the lender has internal guidelines that limit the value.

INITIAL PRINCIPAL LIMIT

As we discussed above, the initial principal limit is the maximum amount that you can get when you first acquire your reverse mortgage, as determined by a combination of the maximum claim amount, the interest rate, and your age.

AGE

The age that matters is the age of the *youngest* borrower. The youngest borrower must be at least 62 years old for HECM loans, and at least 55 for most jumbo loans, with several exceptions (we'll discuss those later).

For now, you need to know that for the purpose of determining your initial principal limit, your age is not exactly your age. The age we will use is the age you were or are going to be on your closest birthday. So, if you turned 70 yesterday, for our purposes you are 70. But if you turned 70 ½ yesterday, you are 71.

Your age impacts your initial principal limit because this is a lifetime loan. The longer you are expected to live the higher your unpaid principal balance will become. So, the younger you are, the less the lender can advance you initially in order to make it unlikely you will ever be underwater. (Owe more than your home is worth.)

INTEREST RATE

We discussed the difference between the initial rate vs. the effective rate. You don't have to make payments on a reverse mortgage, but your interest rate is important for two reasons: The lower your rate, the more you can borrow, and the lower your rate the slower the amount you owe grows, so the less it eats into your equity.

However, you may have to pay more in upfront costs to get that lower interest rate, so there are tradeoffs. Make sure that your reverse mortgage advisor gives you options and helps you understand them.

On a fixed-rate reverse mortgage, the Note rate is the same as the initial rate; it is fixed for the life of the loan.

On an adjustable-rate reverse mortgage, the initial rate is set at the value of the *index* that will be used plus the *margin,* which is defined in your Note.

INDEX

An index is a measure of market interest rates in the same sense that the Dow Jones or the S&P 500 are measures of market stock prices. If you choose an adjustable-rate reverse mortgage, the index is important to you because that index—plus the margin—are what will determine your new interest rate each time it adjusts.

The most common index used today for reverse mortgages is CMT. CMT stands for Constant Maturity Treasuries. The CMT is a value published by the U.S. Treasury based on the yield investors seek to purchase U.S. Treasury bills with a due date of one year later.

CMT is a relatively volatile index, and thus tracks interest rates very closely and quickly, making it an ideal benchmark for lenders to use, since it should closely follow the bank's cost of funds.

MARGIN

The margin is defined in your contract with the lender and is the number that is added to the then-current index value to determine your new interest rate when it is time to adjust. Let's look at an example.

Let's assume the current index is the one-year CMT, it is time for your interest rate to adjust, and the current index value is 3.5 percent.

Let's assume your contract calls for a margin of 3 percent.

To determine your new interest rate, the lender can't just make up a number. They must take the value of the current index (which they don't control) and add the margin (which is set and defined in your Note).

In this case, your new interest rate would be 3.5 percent plus 3 percent = 6.5 percent.

It's that simple.

How do you know if the lender is treating you fairly? You can confirm the index value and margin value yourself.

To confirm the index value, do an internet search for "Current CMT rate" (assuming CMT is your index) and you will find numerous websites that publish the rate every day. Since the rate changes every day, this is useful.

HINT: When comparison shopping for a variable-rate HECM, look at the margin your lender is offering. The lower the margin, the more cash you'll receive and the lower your long-term costs.

PUTTING IT ALL TOGETHER

While it all sounds a bit murky, it's actually quite simple. In a previous section I mentioned that the lender wants their maximum exposure (the amount that you will eventually owe when they expect you to reach your expiration date) to be no more than today's maximum claim amount.

It is uncomfortable for some, but most of us realize that we will not live forever—we have an expiration date. Statistically, lenders know they can predict the *average* expiration date for their borrowers. Based on the youngest borrower's current age, they can predict that—on average—you will no longer need your loan by a certain age because you will have expired. If you do indeed pass away at that time (or at any time for that matter) the loan is due, and they will need to be paid back.

Here's the nugget in this concept:

The lender doesn't want you to owe more than the maximum claim amount when you are likely to expire and, statistically, they can reasonably predict when that is. So, the amount of your equity that you can access today is set so that the money they've lent you plus the accrued unpaid interest will be roughly equal to the maximum claim amount when you pass away.

This is easiest to see visually.

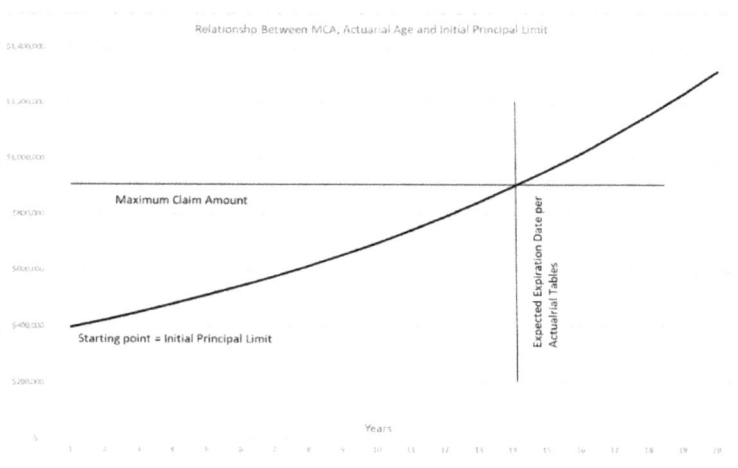

Looking at the illustration above, we assume that we are putting together a HECM loan. The maximum claim amount in this illustration is the appraised value, $900,000. Remember, though, that the maximum claim amount cannot exceed the high-balance conforming loan limit. In 2025, the high-balance conforming loan limit for high-cost areas was $1,209,750; we assume this is a high-cost area.

Since the appraised value is less than that, the maximum claim amount is therefore $900,000.

The youngest borrower is 72 years old, and their actuarial life expectancy is therefore 14 more years. Statistically, the average 72-year-old today will live to 86. If we assume an expected interest rate of 6.5 percent, then the initial principal limit ends up being $372,690 (in this example). Assuming a lump-sum distribution and no payments, the accrued interest would bring the loan balance up to $900,000 in 14 years, when our borrower turns 86.

What happens if our intrepid borrower outlives their actuarial life? Nothing. The loan carries on until you either pass away or move out for more than 12 months. The lender knows that they will be paid off on some loans sooner than their actuarial predictions, and some loans long after. But on average, they will be repaid—with interest—as the actuarial tables predict.

AN IMPORTANT NOTE: Just because in 14 years you will owe as much as the maximum claim amount doesn't mean you have no equity. Your home is *probably* appreciating. If we assume the value of your home is $900,000 today and it is appreciating at 4% per year, then your home would be worth $1,558,509 by your actuarial expiration date. You will owe $900,000, so you will probably still have equity. (This cannot be guaranteed, of course.)

CHAPTER 6

What Can You
Do With the Cash?

ANYTHING YOU WANT! Well, almost anything. You must first use the cash to pay for your mandatory charges, such as paying off existing mortgages and paying closing costs. Once those are paid, the remaining funds are yours to do with as you please; you have converted equity in your home (which belonged to you) to cash (which belongs to you.)

However, you will sign several disclosures advising you **not** to buy an annuity with the proceeds of your reverse mortgage, so this one area is worth discussing.

Prior to the financial crisis and the subsequent more rigorous regulation of the reverse mortgage industry, some reverse mortgage originators were working hand-in-hand with annuity salespeople.

The reverse mortgage salesperson would convince a senior to convert their equity, which was not liquid, into cash. The annuity salesperson would then convince the senior to use that cash to buy an annuity, which is also not liquid. In the exchanges, some pretty darn big commissions were earned, and an awful lot of equity evaporated.

This book is not about whether annuities are good investments for seniors. I'm not an investment advisor and I don't know your personal circumstances. However, I do know you will sign numerous disclosures when getting a reverse mortgage advising you not to buy annuities with the proceeds of the reverse mortgage, and it seems like a good idea to follow that advice.

PURCHASE A HOME

This surprises most folks, but you can use a reverse mortgage to purchase a home. They are not just for refinances anymore! Why would you do this?

Many seniors downsize once they retire. They are looking for a smaller home, or may want to move to a less expensive area, or move closer to their children. However, qualifying for a home mortgage after retirement can be difficult, since most people have considerably less income after retirement than they did before. So, how do you solve this challenge?

If you don't have enough money to pay cash for your new home and can't qualify for a conventional mortgage, a reverse mortgage might open up your options considerably by increasing your buying power—a lot.

If you have plenty of cash to buy the house you want but would prefer to keep some of it liquid for investments or emergencies, a reverse mortgage helps you conserve a large portion of your cash to use as you wish.

Finally, if you have plenty of cash and don't mind committing it to purchasing your new home, setting up a HECM equity line allows you to start with no balance on your reverse mortgage, but gain fast access to your equity and convert it to cash in the event you need it.

If you are not looking to buy a new home and just want to use a reverse mortgage for your existing home, you have a lot of options as to what to do with the money.

PAY BILLS

This is boring, but many reverse mortgage clients end up using the proceeds of their reverse mortgages to pay bills. If you have unpaid bills, of course you'll want to do that. If you have large credit card debt it probably makes sense to pay that off, as the interest rate on your reverse mortgage is almost certainly lower—*much lower*—than the interest rate on your credit cards.

If you are in this situation, you should meet with a trusted advisor or family member to determine what course of action is best for you.

ENJOY LIFE

Well, who doesn't want to enjoy life? They call the "golden decades" the "go-go 60s," the "slow-go 70s," and the "no-go 80s." While I don't know if this is always true, we all want to enjoy life while we still have the energy, strength and health to do so. Of the many options, you might…

TRAVEL

Is there somewhere you've always dreamed of visiting, but you never got around to it? If you have travel destinations on your bucket list, converting some of your home's equity into seeing the world might be an excellent choice.

VACATIONS

Some folks have never taken a cruise or gone to an all-inclusive resort. If this has always been your dream, then yes, you can use the proceeds of a reverse mortgage to realize this dream.

Dinners out and Entertainment

I had one client who had not eaten dinner out at a restaurant for several years when we met. The first thing he wanted to do after we closed on his reverse mortgage was go out to a steak dinner. It wasn't a super fancy place, but at his insistence I joined him, and the steak was outstanding. (Actually, I had a prime rib; he had a tri-tip.)

The point is, sometimes out of necessity we deny ourselves little pleasures, just so that we have enough to eat at all. If we are sitting on tens—or hundreds—of thousands of dollars of idle equity, maybe we can allow ourselves a little guilty pleasure once in a while after we've converted that equity into cash flow.

One client I worked with had not seen a live theater performance in years when we met. She was an artist and loved all the arts. After her reverse mortgage closed, the first thing she did was to go see a live theater production in Berkeley, California. She raved about the experience in an email to me, thanking me for making it happen.

BUY SOMETHING YOU'VE BEEN DENYING YOURSELF

BOAT

I'll get personal here. I'm a sailor, so this would undoubtedly be my first instinct. Many folks dream of owning a boat one day. When you are retired and can actually use it is the perfect time to do so. But boats cost money—to buy, to store, to insure and to maintain. If this is your dream, too, then a reverse mortgage could be the way to use your home's equity to live your dream.

RV

Many retirees buy a recreational vehicle and hit the road to explore places they've never been able to. With RV parking and senior discounts at state and national parks across the country, this could be one of the cheapest ways to see the country. But it costs something, and your reverse mortgage could help you get there.

SECOND HOME

Have you always wanted a vacation home? The two things that stop most folks from realizing this dream are the down payment and qualifying for the mortgage on your second home while still paying a mortgage on your personal residence.

You can use a reverse mortgage to eliminate the payment on your personal residence and to pull enough cash out for a sizable down payment for the second home. You can then finance the rest of the second-home purchase with a conventional mortgage if you qualify. This works particularly well if the vacation home can be rented out when you're not using it.

Hello, condo in Hawaii!

EMERGENCIES

This might be the most common reason folks get a reverse mortgage. Most Americans are only one financial crisis away from bankruptcy.

In particular, older Americans face large medical bills from time to time. While many declare bankruptcy, that may work only once, if at all. As a result, many folks use a reverse mortgage structured as an equity line to eliminate their current mortgage payment while setting up an equity line they can tap to pay unexpected bills when they arise.

SUCCESS STORY

One couple came to me for help with medical bills. They had lived in their home for 40 years and raised their children there. They had paid off their home and then taken out a small conventional equity line, which they used sparingly.

But then the husband (we'll call him "Don") had a stroke. He recovered, but the medical bills wiped out the bank equity line quickly. They asked the bank for an increase in the credit limit, but were turned down because of lack of income.

With bills piling up, they were told their only option was to sell their home. Instead, they turned to me for a HECM set up as a lump sum/equity line combination. They paid off their conventional equity line and their medical bills, and now had an equity line to draw from that they would never have to make payments on.

Don had several more strokes, and sadly, passed away. The wife ("Alice") is very healthy and will probably live for a long time and should be able to stay in the house until she passes away. She has her children and grandchildren over all the time and will be able to continue enjoying her house as long as she wants.

Here is the kicker: If they had sold their home, they would have had a capital gain of close to $700,000. Even with an exemption of $500,000 for a personal residence (see your tax advisor) they would have had a tax bill for a $200,000 gain— after being forced to sell their home!

Instead, the value of their home has gone up *another* $1 million since they took out their reverse mortgage.

But wait—there's more. Based on current tax law as of this writing, if Alice passes away while still in the house, her heirs will inherit the house at a cost basis of whatever the value is at that time. If they sell it immediately, their capital gain will be zero, and they will pay no capital gains taxes. (See your tax advisor for current law and how it applies to your personal situation.) This would save them a capital gains tax bill on $1.2 million in income.

So, Alice and Don got to keep their home and enjoy appreciation, plus their heirs may avoid a huge tax bill entirely. Something to think about.

If you are concerned about how you would handle emergencies should they arise, a reverse mortgage line of credit could bring you the ability to handle unexpected bills, and, more important, peace of mind.

INVESTMENT AND CASH MANAGEMENT TOOL

Ask your financial advisor if you should sell stock when the stock market corrects and goes down a little. They will tell you "No."

But what if you have most of your assets tied up in stocks or mutual funds and are relying on withdrawals for living expenses? A reverse mortgage set up as an equity line could provide money for living expenses and allow you to defer withdrawals until the market recovers. When it does, *then* you can sell your stock and pay off the equity line, freeing it up again for later use.

Most financial advisors do not know about this aspect of reverse mortgages. If you find yourself in this situation, ask your financial advisor about a reverse mortgage option.

RETIRE EARLY

It won't be very early, since in most cases you have to be 62 to qualify for a reverse mortgage. (See Chapter 7, Qualifying.) But if you have had enough of work and are only continuing to work because you need the money to pay your mortgage, consider a lump-sum reverse mortgage to pay it off and drop your monthly payment to zero.

Will that get you to retirement now? It might.

DELAY TAKING SOCIAL SECURITY

The longer you wait to take Social Security, the more you will receive each month in SSI benefits. For most baby boomers, the retirement age is between 66 and 67 for full retirement benefits. If you wait until 70 to begin collecting, you'll receive even more. Whenever you retire, you'll receive benefits only until you die. So, the great gamble for seniors is to guess when the optimal time is to begin taking Social Security benefits.

If you calculate that it's better to wait until full retirement age or even longer, a reverse mortgage could help you get through the years between when you retire and when you begin collecting benefits.

BUT – DON'T INVEST IN ANNUITIES

As we said before, do not use your proceeds to buy an annuity. We won't nag—just don't do it.

HOME HEALTH CARE

Many folks want to remain in their homes as long as possible. Many are determined to live in their homes until they're gone. My mother swore she would leave her home only "when she was carried out in a box," and we worked hard to see that she got her wish.

Home health care for the elderly can be extraordinarily expensive, especially once a senior becomes ill. In our family we were able to handle the load ourselves, but then I had five siblings. Even so, the 24-hour care took a toll on us. It was *not* easy.

Today, since large families are less common, professional in-home supportive care has become widely available. But it's expensive. The average cost of in-home care in 2024 was $24 per hour. For a 44-hour week, that adds up to $55,000 per year. For round-the-clock care (which my parents both needed) the cost would be more than $200,000 per year. In high-cost areas, it's even more.

I have worked with several families who used a reverse mortgage to fund in-home care. The monthly payment option can work well for this. It is rarely enough for all the needed care, but it can supplement other income to help pay for it. For families who choose a blend of family care and professional in-home care, it might be enough to pay for all that they need.

Finally, you might remember that if a senior is able to remain in their home until they're gone, their home is passed on to their heirs without any capital gains. (Ask your financial advisor about your particular situation, though.) For seniors who wish to leave as much as possible to their children, using a reverse mortgage for in-home care achieves two goals simultaneously.

CHAPTER 7

QUALIFYING

WHAT DOES IT TAKE to qualify for a reverse mortgage? It takes more than just a lot of equity. Regulators have created rules and guidelines to make the product safer for seniors. Their goal has been to make sure that seniors are not forced to sell their homes because of a reverse mortgage. These rules have, in general, been very good for consumers, and lenders must follow them, so they are worth reviewing.

PERSONAL RESIDENCE

You can only get a reverse mortgage on your personal (primary) residence. This means you must live in the property. The lender will examine your credit report, tax returns and possibly other documents, such as your mortgage statement, to verify that the home is indeed your personal residence. Do your tax returns show the property as your residence? Are your bills mailed to this address? If the answer to either of these questions is "no," you *may* not be eligible for a reverse mortgage.

As a rule, for a property to qualify as your primary residence, you must inhabit the home for at least six months plus one day each calendar year.

After you get a reverse mortgage, you must continue to live in the home for as long as you want to keep it. If you move out permanently, or if you move out even temporarily for more than 12 months, the loan will be called, meaning it is due and payable in full.

ESTABLISH MAXIMUM CLAIM AMOUNT

You must have equity in the property, as we discussed in Chapter 5 *How Much Can You Get?* This is established using either the appraised value or, in the case of a HECM, the conforming loan limit for your area if it is less than the appraised value.

The point is that you must have quite a lot of equity to support the new reverse mortgage to qualify.

AGE

You must be 62 or older to qualify for a HECM reverse mortgage. However, there are exceptions. A n*on-borrowing spouse* can be any age as long as they are old enough to legally execute a contract. However, a younger non-borrowing spouse will reduce the initial principal limit available.

Many jumbo lenders are also now accepting borrowers as young as 55 as a primary borrower on the loan, and this may go even lower in the future.

Interestingly, there is no upper limit on age.

INCOME

Although you do not need to make payments on your mortgage, you must have enough income to pay the expenses that the reverse mortgage doesn't cover, such as property taxes, homeowner's insurance, HOA dues and property maintenance. In addition, you'll need to cover any monthly obligations on your credit report, such as credit cards, car loans, and student loans. Do seniors have student loans? Yes, some do.

Once those expenses are covered, you still need a little more income, because you'll have some living expenses. The amount that you'll need to document depends on where you live in the country, and it changes over time. Your loan officer should be able to assess your verifiable income and let you know if you qualify.

WHAT KIND OF INCOME COUNTS?

The most common type of income for seniors is Social Security Income, of course. Other types of income that count toward qualifying for your mortgage are:

- Employment income (if it is expected to continue).
- Pensions.
- IRA withdrawals (if they are expected to continue).
- Annuities.
- Rental income, whether from an auxiliary unit (granny unit or in-law quarters) on your property or from another property.
- Business income (if it is expected to continue).
- Dividend or income from notes (if it is expected to continue).

You get the idea. If you have income from any source, and if we can document that you are likely to continue receiving it, we can probably count it.

HOW DO YOU DOCUMENT INCOME?

Social Security retirement benefits are super easy. We need the SSA award letter that you receive each year and a couple of months of bank statements documenting its receipt. Sometimes your previous year's 1099 statement from Social Security will substitute for bank statements.

Employment income is also easy, as we need just a W2 and paystubs. However, your employer must certify in a written verification of employment that they expect your employment to continue.

Pension income is usually documented by something like an award letter that you received when you started drawing the pension, plus a couple of months of bank statements to document receipt. If you receive paper checks in the mail, we'll want to see copies of those.

IRA withdrawals and annuity payments are documented with both bank statements and statements from your IRA account. The IRA (or annuity) statements will document the withdrawals, and the bank statements will document the deposits.

Rental income is documented with tax returns. You declare your income and expenses to the IRS on your Schedule E of your return.

Business income is the same, except you declare business income either on your Schedule C or, if it's a partnership, a K-1.

Dividend or Note income is also declared to the IRS.

I'm sure you see a pattern here. We simply need to document that you actually receive the income you tell us you are receiving, and that we can reasonably expect that income to continue. Because you need to document so little income (compared with a conventional mortgage), the vast majority of homeowners qualify easily.

ASSETS

Unlike a conventional mortgage, you don't need assets in the bank to qualify for a reverse mortgage. However, we will ask you for two consecutive, recent bank statements, to make sure you have enough money to close the loan, and to document the account to which your payments will be sent.

CREDIT

You don't need perfect credit, but we need to know what your monthly bills are. Your credit report will tell us whether you have credit card bills or installment loans, like a car loan, that require monthly payments. If your monthly bills are so high that you can't qualify with your current income, you may be able to pay off these bills in escrow and close out those cards to help you qualify. You will need enough equity so that your initial principal limit covers these costs.

We will also see if you have any tax liens, collections or judgments that need to be paid off when the reverse mortgage closes.

If there is enough room in your initial principal limit, you can pay off all liens in escrow. If there is not, you may not qualify unless you can come up with the cash to pay off the extra mandatory charges in escrow.

PROPERTY

Your property has to meet some guidelines, too, for you to qualify for a reverse mortgage.

For HECM loans, your property must meet Federal Housing Administration guidelines. FHA has more stringent guidelines than those for conventional loans because the U.S. Department of Housing and Urban Development (HUD) promises to buy the loan from the lender if you ever owe more than the home is worth.

This is particularly risky for reverse mortgages, because the date that the lender will face this issue is unknown, and a lot can happen over the years. Consequently, FHA wants to make sure that the property is protected against risks that could cause damage to the property.

In general, FHA wants to make sure the property is *safe* for inhabitants and guests, *sound,* meaning it is protected against damage, and *secure,* meaning that the lender's security interest in the property will have value if a lender takes it back.

In practice, this means:

- Stairs and any difference in levels over three feet must have handrails.
- Windows and doors must be intact and operable.
- There can be no plumbing leaks.
- Floor surfaces must be serviceable and marketable.
- Any wood-destroying pests must be eliminated.
- Trip hazards must be eliminated.
- The electrical box and wiring must be up to code and wiring must be in serviceable condition.
- All rooms must have a heat source.
- The roof must be intact and functioning.
- The water heater must meet local code requirements.
- The driveway and street must have all-weather access for emergency vehicles.
- Bathrooms must have a toilet, sink and shower and be functional.

In essence, all major components of your home must be functional, and any structural or functional deficiency that could lead to damage in the future must be corrected before you can close on your reverse mortgage.

Lenders of non-HECM reverse mortgages may be more flexible if they choose, but most will follow FHA guidelines.

In addition to these guidelines, your property:

- Must be a one-unit single-family home, although you can have one auxiliary unit.

- Can be a detached single-family house, a condo, a planned unit development or a manufactured home.

- If it is a condo, it must be in an FHA-approved project to do a HECM loan.

- If it is a manufactured home, it must be permanently affixed on land you own.

- Must be no more than 10 acres for a HECM loan.

- Must be no more than 20 acres for a non-HECM loan, although exceptions are possible.

This list is not all-inclusive, and lenders can add additional requirements. In general, remember that once you get a reverse mortgage, someone else now has an interest in keeping your home in good working order. In the long run, this benefits you as well as the lender, because your home will be well cared for, retain its value and remain a safe place for you to live as long as you want.

CHAPTER 8

COSTS

MOST OF THE COSTS of a reverse mortgage are similar to those of a forward mortgage, but there are exceptions. Many of these fees vary by region, so I won't try to guess how much you will be charged, but I will give you a list of fees you are likely to be charged and explain what they are for, and how you might be able to reduce them.

For each charge, I'll let you know who charges the fee and what it is you are getting for what you are paying.

COUNSELING FEE

This is one fee that you will not have to pay on most conventional mortgages, but it must be paid on a reverse mortgage. In order to stop abusive practices and to protect seniors, FHA requires anyone getting a reverse mortgage to receive counseling after getting a proposal for a reverse mortgage.

Who charges the fee? You will be given a list of HUD-approved independent counseling agencies who do not have an interest in the transaction, and who are not affiliated with the lender. You may choose any counselor you wish, and you can do your counseling in person or over the phone. The counselors are located all over the country and there may not be one close enough for you to do in-person counseling, however.

The counseling agency will charge you for the counseling

session and a certificate of completion. The fee varies, but it is one of the smaller charges for the loan. In most cases, you will need to pay this fee when you receive counseling, whether or not you go through with your loan.

What do you get for it? You get about an hour or so with a financial counselor who understands reverse mortgages. They will ask you a series of questions to make sure that you understand what you are getting, and you may ask them questions if there is anything you don't understand.

UPFRONT MORTGAGE INSURANCE PREMIUM

If you are getting a HECM loan you will be required to pay mortgage insurance in two ways: an upfront charge in escrow, and an annual mortgage insurance premium, which will be divided up and charged each month to you along with interest.

The upfront mortgage insurance premium is the largest single line item charge for the loan for most borrowers. It is based on your maximum claim amount, which as you may recall from Chapter 5 *How Much Can You Get?* is either your appraised value or the conforming loan limit for your county, whichever is less.

Who charges the fee? HUD (Housing and Urban Development, the parent agency of FHA) charges the fee. Neither the lender nor your mortgage broker gets any portion of this fee, and it cannot be waived or negotiated. The only way to avoid it is to get a proprietary (jumbo) reverse mortgage, if that is a feasible option for you.

What do you get for it? FHA ensures the lender that they will be reimbursed losses if they end up taking the home back and there is not enough equity to pay back all the lender's outlays plus interest. So, you get two benefits for this fee:

1. Because lenders have less risk if the loan is FHA-insured, they are willing to give you a higher initial principal limit and a lower interest rate than they otherwise would.

2. If you are ever "underwater," FHA will purchase the loan from the lender. When you die, your heirs will have the option to purchase the family home from FHA for 95% of its current value, even if you owe much more than that.

It's important to point out, however, that **all** reverse mortgages are non-recourse loans, meaning that the lender can never come after you for a deficiency if you owe more than what the home is worth. Even jumbo loans, which do not have mortgage insurance, are non-recourse loans. However, because of the risk to the lender, jumbo loans tend to be a little more conservative in terms of how much money you can get, and the interest rate tends to be higher.

ORIGINATION FEE

You may, or may not, pay an origination fee. For a HECM loan there is a limit on how much you can be charged, depending on your initial principal limit.

Who charges the fee? Your lender will charge your origination fee.

What do you get for it? You get your loan for this fee. This pays for the efforts of your origination team: processor, underwriter, and other administrative functions.

What you should know about this. The origination fee for most reverse mortgages is set by the lender, and in most cases is not negotiable. However, that isn't always the case, depending on the loan program you choose, so when you comparison shop for your reverse mortgage, ask your lender (whether working with a broker or a direct lender) these two questions:

- Is this fee negotiable?
- Can you give me a credit in escrow to cover this fee?

The answer will usually be "no," but at least you asked.

LENDER FEES

The lenders will charge fees for specific services rendered. You *may* be able to negotiate these fees a little, but there will be little (or usually no) wiggle room. (On the other hand, you may be able to ask for a credit from the lender or your broker to cover the fees.)

Lender fees might include processing, document prep, attorney trust review, and other minor fees.

APPRAISAL

The appraiser will be working from a fee schedule and would not normally reduce their fee. However, lenders must order their appraisal through an independent appraisal management company (known as an AMC). Some AMCs will have lower fees than others, so ask your lender if there is a difference in fees between the AMCs available to them and, if they are not using the lowest priced, why not?

NOTE: Speed might matter more than price, and quality always does, so the lowest priced appraisal company is not always the best choice.

CREDIT REPORT

Some lenders will pay for your credit report in advance. Most who do will charge you for it in escrow, and some will have you pay for it up front with your credit card.

Who charges the fee? Your broker or lender runs the credit report, but it is paid to a third party called a credit agency. The agencies collect data from the three credit bureaus and consolidate the information into a credit report. The information in the report belongs to the bureaus, the report itself belongs to the credit agency (because it's proprietary), and you have some clearly delineated rights to see some of the information— enough to correct inaccurate information, if there is any.

What do you get for it? You get a disclosure that shows your credit score and your creditors, so you can take action to correct inaccurate data. The lender gets a report that tells them what you owe, to whom, and if you've paid them back as promised.

What you should know about this. This is a very small fee, so while it's not negotiable it's not very material. The lender **cannot** charge you more than the actual cost of the third-party fees for providing the report.

FLOOD CERTIFICATION

Who charges the fee? Your lender charges this fee to cover the actual charge for a service that checks to see if your property is located in a FEMA-designated flood zone.

What do you get for it? If you are in a flood zone, flood insurance will be required. If you are not in a flood zone, flood insurance is not required. So, this is important information.

What you should know about this. Like credit reports, the lender charges this fee but is not allowed to charge you more than the actual cost.

MERS FEE

Who charges the fee? Your lender charges this fee to pay a company known as Mortgage Electronic Registration Systems (MERS) to register and track ownership of your loan through its lifetime. Lenders may sell loans from time to time, and only the legal owner at any point in time may foreclose, so it's important to be able to prove who owns a loan.

Think of this as the equivalent of the county recorder tracking ownership of real estate, except it is nationwide, and tracks ownership of your mortgage.

What do you get for it? No lender will make a loan without this today, so this fee enables you to get your loan.

What you should know about this. This fee is not negotiable, but the lender can only charge you the actual cost.

Underwriting/Administration

Who charges the fee? This is a fee that your lender charges. It might be called an *underwriting* fee, or an *administration or admin* fee.

What do you get for it? Your loan is reviewed by a highly qualified underwriter to confirm that it meets the guidelines of the program to which you have applied.

What you should know about this. This fee is rarely negotiable, but it does vary a bit from one lender to another. Also, look for duplicate fees. For instance, if a lender charges you an underwriting fee **and** an administration fee or an application fee, they may be trying to charge twice for the same service.

If you are working with a broker, it will be the lender, not the broker, who charges this fee.

PROCESSING

Who charges the fee? If you are working with a broker, the broker may charge you this fee. If you are working directly with the lender, it will be the lender. For many reverse mortgage products, a broker cannot charge this fee to you.

What do you get for it? No matter who you work with, someone is responsible for gathering your documents, making sure they are sufficient for the underwriting guidelines of the loan program you are seeking, and putting them into the proper order for the underwriter.

What you should know about this. This fee may be negotiable. It does pay for actual service from an actual person, who may be a direct employee of the broker or lender, or who may be an independent third-party processor. However, the fee varies from lender to lender, and your lender might be willing to negotiate this fee.

DOC PREP

Who charges the fee? Your lender charges this fee.

What do you get for it? The lender must prepare your document package for signing. This is an extensive package with lots of details that must be right, so most lenders will charge you to pay for this person (who might be an internal employee or a third party.)

What you should know about this. This fee will vary from one lender to another. It's usually a relatively minor fee, so it's not one of the fees you would typically make a fuss over.

CONDO (HOA) CERTIFICATION

Who charges the fee? Your HOA (or HOA management company) charges this fee.

What do you get for it? If you live in a condominium, you may be required to provide a condominium questionnaire and certification. This is a form that your HOA prepares for the lender, which documents the financial health of your association. The survey will reveal things like how many units are in the HOA, how many are rentals, how many are behind on their dues, and what the monthly dues are. This helps the lender verify that factors outside of your control do not increase their risk.

What you should know about this. The lender may only pass on the actual cost of the HOA cert, so this fee is not negotiable as a rule. Many HOAs will also ask for advance payment to prepare this form, so you may end up paying for this fee in advance.

TITLE/ESCROW FEES

Escrow and title are separate functions but in many areas are handled by the same company, so we'll examine these fees together.

SETTLEMENT/CLOSING

Who charges the fee? Your escrow company charges this fee.

What do you get for it? An escrow company is a neutral third party that collects documentation and money and completes the transaction in accordance with mutually agreed upon instructions, so this fee pays for this specific service.

What you should know about this. Escrow companies work from a published fee schedule, although lenders can negotiate with escrow companies for special pricing. While this fee is not negotiable between you and the lender, the fee will vary among escrow companies, so if the lender uses an escrow company with a higher fee than others you are considering, ask if there is a less expensive alternative.

Be aware, however, that sometimes a company that charges a lower escrow fee charges a higher title insurance premium, so the total fees for title and escrow are more important than individual line items.

OWNER'S TITLE INSURANCE

Who charges the fee? Your title insurance company charges this fee. In many areas, the title company and escrow company are one.

What do you get for it? When you purchase a home, you want to make sure that you are buying exactly what you think you are buying. It's not as simple as you think. There could be old liens against the property that you don't know about that you inherit with the property, or your neighbor might have improvements encroaching on your property (or you on theirs). There are many issues that could crop up which could negatively affect your ownership interests.

A title insurance company researches the history of your property when you buy it, and then provides an insurance policy that covers fixing any issues they might have missed. This policy, in effect, is insurance that you are buying exactly what you think you are buying.

What you should know about this. You will only be charged this fee if you are buying a property. You will not be charged this fee if you are getting a reverse mortgage for a property you already own. If you are purchasing a property, owner's title insurance is optional by law. However, no lender will make a loan without it, since what protects you also protects them. If you decide you want a reverse mortgage on your new home, you will be required to purchase this policy.

LENDER'S TITLE INSURANCE

Who charges the fee? Your title insurance company charges this fee.

What do you get for it? When you get a mortgage (any mortgage, whether reverse or forward), the lender wants to make sure that they are secured by their collateral (your home) exactly in the way they think they are. This means—just as with an owner's policy—they want to make sure there are no claims against the property that could diminish the value of their collateral (for example, tax liens).

This policy ensures the lender that, if any issues arise, the title insurance company will take care of those issues. It protects you as well as the lender from claims that you are not aware of.

What you should know about this. Like the escrow fee, this fee comes from a published fee schedule. Fees vary from one title company to another, but are generally not negotiable. The escrow fee and lender's title insurance are the two largest charges for title and escrow, and while different companies have different strategies the total of the two are usually pretty close for most companies. Therefore, when comparing offers, pay attention to the sum of the title and escrow fees rather than trying to negotiate individual line items.

NOTARY FEE

Who charges the fee? Your title insurance company charges this fee.

What do you get for it? When you sign your final loan documents a notary must be present to confirm your identity. This protects you and the lender against fraud by preventing someone pretending to be you from getting financing on your home. (Yes, that happens.)

What you should know about this. You may only be charged the actual fee. Notary fees are minor compared to all the other fees and are as a rule not negotiable anyway. Also, the quality of notaries varies. Since these are the people who will be explaining very important documents to you, the cheapest notary is rarely the best choice. In short, don't sweat this fee.

COURIER

Who charges the fee? Your title insurance company charges this fee.

What do you get for it? There may be paper files being sent back and forth via a secure service. This happens less and less, but with reverse mortgages it is still common.

What you should know about this. You can only be charged the actual fee for the service if it's provided by a third party. It's a minor fee, and not all lenders charge for it.

GOVERNMENT / RECORDING FEES

The county recorder must record your mortgage or trust deed, and grant deeds if applicable. The county assessor needs to review the transaction to see if it affects the assessed value of your property, and therefore your property taxes.

TRANSFER TAXES / TAX STAMPS

Transfer taxes are charged in most counties in the United States on purchase transactions only. These are often referred to alternatively as tax stamps. The amount of the tax will depend on the transaction price and your county.

Some counties charge taxes on new mortgages, so you may see an estimated tax stamp charge in your reverse mortgage proposal even if you are only getting a mortgage.

RECORDING FEES

Who charges the fee? The county recorder charges this fee.

What do you get for it? The county recorder officially records every transaction related to real estate in their county. This includes grant deeds (the document used to buy, sell or transfer your property) and mortgages or trust deeds for financing. By having an official record, your interests in the property (and the lender's interests) are protected because they are a matter of public record and therefore can be proven.

What you should know about this. You can only be charged the actual fee for the service, and of course it is not negotiable.

SUMMARY

These are the fees you are most likely to see when you get a reverse mortgage. Depending on your circumstances and where you live, there may be others, such as attorney's fees and survey costs, for example. You may have to pay some costs before you close escrow, but most will only be charged only if you are successful in getting your mortgage. In general, if a fee is not collected at the time the service is performed, you won't pay it unless you close.Chapter 9 Shopping for the Best Deal

Like conventional mortgages, reverse mortgages are all eventually sold to the same small number of investors. Because of this, the fundamental structure and offer of most reverse mortgages are about the same. However, there can be small differences in terms, and fairly large differences in certain costs, so it pays to comparison shop.

COMPARISON SHOP

Yes, you can shop for your reverse mortgage! The disclosure package lenders send you, however, is massive, and contains far too much information for the average homeowner to be able to sort out their options. Here are some tools to help you identify the pages that are most important to you, and how to compare the offers.

You want to look for the two or three most important pages in your proposal package. Here's what you are looking for:

First, review the line item detailed estimates of the origination costs of the loan. It will look something like this:

Estimated Closing Costs

Finance Charges

Appraisal Admin Fee

Document preparation

Final Appraisal Inspection

Flood certification

HECM counseling fee

MERS registration

Origination Fee

Repair administration

Settlement or closing fee

Sub Escrow Fee

Other Charges

Appraisal fee

Credit report

Lender's title insurance

Recording charges mortgage

Recording Service Fee

Tax Cert Fee

Tax service

Total Estimated Settlement Costs

NOTE: I have left out any actual figures here because they will vary greatly depending on your location, circumstances and lender you choose. Knowing what form to look for in your disclosure package will save you a lot of time and aggravation. Understanding how to read this form will help you compare lenders and negotiate the best deal.

While all the costs were discussed in detail in the last chapter, you need to know something important about broker compensation.

BROKER COMPENSATION/LENDER CREDIT

All lenders pay someone to counsel you and bring in the loan. They will either pay their own staff or, like a cruise line that hires a travel agent, engage brokers to find and bring in clients for them. Most reverse mortgage lenders do both—they have their own internal staff, and they pay brokers the same as they would have to pay their own internal people.

If you go directly to a lender there will be no line item for broker compensation. They are not required to disclose their payments to their own internal staff. If you go to a broker, there will be another line item in this grid for broker compensation, and you get to see exactly how much they pay someone to originate your loan.

However, broker compensation isn't set in most cases until your loan is ready to close. Charges in escrow cannot be more than what you've been quoted in the initial proposal. Most brokers, therefore, enter a very high number for this. The key thing to remember is that you don't pay the broker compensation, and it's almost always going to be less than the quote in the disclosure. Ask your broker, if you use one, to verify this.

If you work with a lender directly, you won't see this because lenders are not required to disclosure this information—only brokers must do so.

There are a couple of important points here. As we discussed in the last chapter, the compensation to your loan advisor (whether a broker or an employee of the lender) varies a lot. In certain cases, the amount of compensation might be large enough that you can negotiate with the originator to use some of it to pay some of your closing costs.

Having said that, keep in mind that a reverse mortgage is a more complex financial product than a conventional mortgage. Reverse mortgage brokers have to complete extra training in order to be able to offer the product, and devote a lot more time than with a conventional mortgage. Nobody works for free. The amount of compensation might seem large to you, but your reverse mortgage advisor does need to make higher commissions on reverse mortgages to justify the cost of the extra training and time spent helping you choose the right product for your family and helping you understand how it will impact your financial picture.

The bottom line: Pay attention to this line to see whether there might be an opportunity to ask your mortgage advisor to pay some or all of your loan costs. Ask all the loan officers you speak with to see who offers you the best deal.

ADVICE IS GOLDEN

Now I will contradict myself a bit. While price is important, once you've let all your suitors know that you are shopping and have asked them for their best offer, the pricing and the terms should all be pretty close.

Once you've reached this point, keep in mind that with a financial product this complex, *advice is golden*. But *GREAT advice is diamond-studded platinum*. Choosing the right reverse mortgage product is about more than just getting the best price.

You want to be sure your advisor does all of the following:

- Asks you about your short-range, medium-range and long-term plans.

- Takes the time to understand your particular needs and concerns.

- Has access to all the available products that might be useful for you.
- Has a deep understanding of the benefits, costs and risks of each.
- *Teaches and informs you.* You should know enough to be confident you are making a wise, informed decision.

If a mortgage advisor doesn't take the time to understand why you are considering a reverse mortgage and what you are trying to accomplish, drop them.

If a reverse mortgage specialist doesn't discuss the myriad possible products that might be relevant to your goals, circumstances and concerns, drop them.

If your loan officer only has one or two products to offer, drop them.

If your reverse mortgage advisor seems confused about how a product works, or its implications for your future, or can't confidently answer your questions, drop them.

If you don't feel like you've learned anything from your loan officer, or if what they tell you turns out to be false, drop them.

In short, you are looking for a competent, ethical professional who cares as much about your future as they do about their commission. If you pay attention to how they act and what they say, you'll know.

BROKER VS. DIRECT

I'll leave you with one final word on shopping for the best deal. You can choose to work with a broker or a direct lender. Brokers do not, as a rule, add any cost to a reverse mortgage, and they certainly won't if you shop aggressively.

I prefer to remain in the broker role because it gives me access to more products and, since lenders know they have to compete for our business, and I can almost always offer *slightly* better pricing for you. In addition, more intense training is required to be qualified to do reverse mortgages as a broker, so the training is more thorough, more robust.

While lenders' inside salespeople are paid by the company, brokers are not paid unless you are happy enough with the product and service to close the loan. Although the lenders pay us, *you* are the one who controls whether we get paid or not. We want you to be happy.

A lender-employed reverse mortgage loan officer, however, might be perfectly well-equipped, too. Just make sure that you ask plenty of questions, because they are managed directly by their employers, and are paid to move products rather than advise you.

CHAPTER 9

WHAT TO EXPECT
FROM THE PROCESS

THE PROCESS OF GETTING a reverse mortgage differs from that of getting a conventional mortgage in several notable ways. Most of these differences relate to rules meant to protect seniors from bad advice and bad decisions. Reverse mortgages require more disclosures, more forms to sign and more steps. This chapter will help you understand what you can expect.

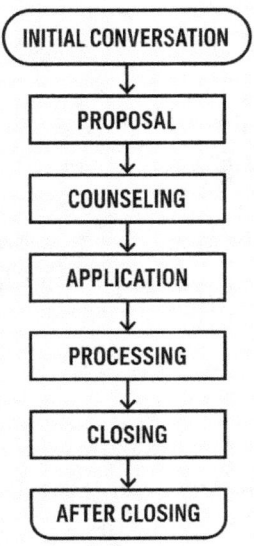

INITIAL CONVERSATION

When you first contact a reverse mortgage advisor you will need to provide four key pieces of information: Your birth dates, your address, the amount owed on your existing mortgage, if any, and your income.

The advisor should ask you a number of other questions as well. If they don't, find another advisor. To properly advise you if you should get a reverse mortgage and which product best suits your circumstances, concerns and goals, we need to know the following:

How long do you want to live in your home?

How much money do you have in savings?

Why do you need extra money? How will you be using it?

If you have an existing mortgage, what are the terms? (Interest rate, fixed or variable, amount of your monthly payment.)

Is there someone in your life (such as children) who might have a strong opinion about you having a reverse mortgage?

Do you have a financial advisor or someone who helps you with decisions about your money?

How is your health?

If you need in-home care now or later on in your life, how do you plan to pay for it?

Not all of these questions may be relevant to your situation, but the answers will help us understand which product would best suit your needs.

PROPOSAL

After this interview we will prepare a proposal for you. In this proposal we will recommend at least three different reverse mortgage products. Your proposal will contain a few mandated forms plus numerous disclosures. The disclosures vary by state.

Their purpose is to help you understand your rights and the terms of the loans being offered.

Be aware that the proposal may be very long and contain dozens of pages. Much of the package is boilerplate. It includes a pamphlet from HUD called "Use Your Home to Stay at Home," and another called "Reverse Mortgage Self-Evaluation: A Checklist of Key Considerations," produced by the National Reverse Mortgage Lenders Association. (NRMLA) These two pamphlets make up the bulk of the package and can be reviewed on our own without your lender present.

COUNSELING

Once you have your proposal in hand you must attend counseling before we can move forward.

Your proposal will include a list of counseling agencies across the country and include those which are closest to you. We cannot recommend which agency you choose. These agencies are independent organizations approved by HUD to provide reverse mortgage counseling. Their mission is to make sure you understand how a reverse mortgage will impact you and your family. They will ask you questions to be sure that you do, and answer any questions you may have.

Once you choose your counseling agency you want to make your appointment as soon as possible, as they are often booked up and it may take a few days to get one. Most agencies charge between $150 and $200 per session, although that fee may be rising soon. Most counseling agencies want you to pay this fee in advance via a credit card. If you cannot pay, ask the agency if they will accept payment in escrow when the loan closes, or if they have any options for low-income borrowers. In no case can your lender pay for this.

Your counseling session will be designed around the specific product you want to apply for. Your counselor will therefore need to see some of the pages in your proposal. Your reverse mortgage advisor should have sent you a separate package along with your proposal in which those pages have been extracted. Either you or your mortgage advisor may provide these forms to the counselor, once you have independently chosen your counseling agency.

WHAT QUESTIONS WILL MY COUNSELOR ASK?

Your counselor will ask you many questions but will almost always ask you the following.

Q: Who owns your home when you get a reverse mortgage?
A: You will still own your home.

Q: What happens to the cash you generate from the reverse mortgage?
A: It goes into your bank account to be used in any manner you want.

Q: Do you have to make payments on a reverse mortgage?
A: No.

Q: Do you have to pay the reverse mortgage back?
A: Yes, when the house is sold the reverse mortgage and accrued interest will be paid back out of escrow.

Q: When is the loan due?
A: After the borrower passes away or is absent from the home for more than 12 months. When it comes due, the lender will give you at least six months to sell the home or pay them back in some other fashion.

Q: Can you default on a reverse mortgage?
A: Yes. You must continue to maintain the home and pay property taxes, insurance and HOA dues on time.

Q: Do you plan to buy an annuity (insurance product) with the proceeds of the loan?
A: You are strongly advised not to buy an annuity with the proceeds of your reverse mortgage.

Your counseling session will last at least an hour and often goes a little over that. You may choose to receive counseling over the phone, in person, or over video chat.

When you have finished your counseling session, the counselor will prepare a counseling certificate and send it to you and your mortgage advisor. Once your counselor sends the certificate out, you must wait a few days before your lender can proceed with your application. The length of the cooling-off period varies by state.

APPLICATION

After your cooling-off period has expired we can proceed with the application. Until this point you have not actually asked your lender for a loan; you've only expressed interest and learned about your options.

Your application will include much of the same forms and information as your proposal. You are now formally requesting your reverse mortgage. You will have the option to cancel the application several more times through the process, but now the process begins. Your lender should walk you through the application to ensure you understand your rights and obligations.

Once you have signed the application, your reverse mortgage advisor will submit your loan for approval.

PROCESSING

The processor is someone who organizes all the forms and documentation that your mortgage advisor has gathered. They review the file to make sure that the information in your application is correct and all of the necessary documentation is in the file.

Once the processor has completed their initial work, they order the appraisal and submit your application to underwriting.

APPRAISAL

The processor orders the appraisal at this point. The appraiser must be an independent, disinterested party. The lender will order the appraisal through an independent company called an appraisal management company (AMC.) AMCs maintain a panel of independent appraisers across the country, so your appraisal will be done by a local appraiser familiar with your city and type of property.

The appraiser must be paid whether your loan closes or not, so the appraisal fee is usually due in advance. Your lender may ask for credit card information at the time of your application, or the AMC may send you a payment link to pay online. Appraisal fees vary across the country. If you have a custom home or one in a rural or mountainous area, your appraisal requires more time on the part of the appraiser, so expect to pay a little more.

If your home is worth more than $2 million a second appraisal is usually required. This appraisal won't be ordered until the first one is completed and underwritten. The second appraisal is paid for by the lender.

UNDERWRITING

The underwriter's job is to review your application and documentation to ensure that you meet the underwriting requirements of the lender and loan program you have chosen. They will make note of any missing information or documents and either deny your loan (which should be very rare), issue a final approval (even more rare), or issue a conditional approval.

A conditional approval is an agreement by the lender to make the loan if certain conditions are satisfied. Most of the conditions are typically house-keeping items that help the lender properly make the loan, follow the laws protecting you, and securitize your home as collateral.

Once the conditional approval is received, your team goes to work to meet all of the conditions. This may involve your mortgage advisor, processor, escrow officer, title officer, and the appraiser. Some conditions may be questions only you can answer. In that case, your mortgage advisor or processor will reach out to you.

After the conditions have been gathered, they are submitted to underwriting. Once reviewed and approved, the underwriter issues a final approval, sometimes called a "clear to close."

CLOSING

Before you can sign any documents that fully commit you to taking the loan, you will be sent a final accounting of the fees associated with the loan and the loan terms. You will have three days to review these documents before signing your loan agreement. During this time, we strongly recommend you review the disclosures and ask questions about anything that you don't understand.

FUNDING

In many states you must wait a few more days before we can fund your loan and send your money. In California we must wait 3 days. Other states vary. Once your cooling-off period expires your lender sends the money and closing instructions to your escrow officer, who records the transaction, pays off any existing mortgages that you have, and sends your money to you. In some states escrow is handled by attorneys rather than escrow officers.

AFTER CLOSING

Within a few weeks you will receive a welcome letter from the company you will be dealing with from here on. You don't have to make payments on a reverse mortgage, but you can if you wish and the lender must let you know each month how much interest was added to your loan balance, how much you now owe, and your current interest rate.

Keep this information in the welcome package handy in case you need to reach out to your lender in the future with questions about your loan.

If you have questions about reverse mortgages in general, your mortgage advisor should be able to answer them or at least point you to the right resources.

CHAPTER 10

WHAT YOU WORRY ABOUT

WILL YOU LOSE THE HOUSE?

LET'S BE HONEST – reverse mortgages got a pretty bad rap back in the day, often with good reason. There were toxic products sold by unscrupulous salesmen, and many seniors were hurt—some even lost their homes. Seniors today are understandably wary about reverse mortgages.

Because of this, many seniors put off getting a reverse mortgage for many years and miss out on the benefits of the product. This is unfortunate, because the financial crisis did a pretty thorough job of cleaning out the bad players in the industry.

YOU STILL OWN YOUR HOME

FHA-insured products (HECMs) in particular are underwritten to stringent FHA guidelines not only in terms of originating the loan, but in terms of what terms and costs a lender is required to offer.

In any reverse mortgage product offered today, *you* will still own your home, and you can live in it as long as you want and are able to. Reverse mortgages are a lifetime product. No one can ever tell you to leave your home until you are ready.

With a reverse mortgage, interest will accrue over time, so your loan balance will grow. However, 100% of the *equity* appreciation belongs to you. If you decide to move out, you can sell the home and take the remaining equity with you. If you pass away while living in the home you can bequeath your home to your heirs, who only have to pay off the reverse mortgage. They can do that by paying cash, refinancing the home with a conventional loan, or selling it. But it's their choice; the home belongs to them.

YOU'LL (PROBABLY) NEVER OWE MORE MONEY THAN YOUR HOME IS WORTH

It's likely your equity will grow rather than decline for the first few years after you get a reverse mortgage. This last concept of how a reverse mortgage affects your equity over time can be a little hard to grasp. It can easily be seen visually, however.

ILLUSTRATION: WHAT HAPPENS TO EQUITY OVER TIME

Let's take a look at a sample case. Assume that the property has a value of $500,000, which, as you know by now, means that

Initial Calculations		
Appraised Value: $	500,000	
Maximum Claim Amount: $	500,000	
Initial Pincipal Limit: $	245,000	
Initial Draw: $	147,000	(Limited to 60% if IPL)
Mandatory Expenses		
Origination Fee: $	3,000	
Other Expenses: $	5,500	
Liens: $	138,500	
Mandatory Expenses: $	147,000	
Paid Out Over 14 Years: $	532.74	Monthly

appraised value will be the maximum claim amount. Our borrower, Mary, wants to pay off her existing mortgage and then receive monthly payments for life.

Her mortgage balance is $138,500. The loan will cost about $8,500, so she will have *mandatory expenses* of $147,000.

Given her age, the actuarial tables estimate she has 14 years left to live. We'll assume an interest rate of 6 percent. The lender offers her $147,000 to pay the mandatory expenses, plus $532.74 per month for the rest of her life. This is just enough so that when her actuarial time is up, she'll owe $500,000, the current appraised value.

If she lives past this, she will still get her monthly income, for as long as she lives. But the lender calculates how much she will get per month based on assumptions about value, the interest rate and the age of the occupant *today*.

If we project out 14 years, her projected actuarial lifespan, we can see that Mary's property will be worth $865,838 and her loan balance will be $509,686, leaving her $356,152 in equity, about the same as $353,000, the equity she had before her reverse mortgage.

Future Equity Analysis					
Projected Loan Balance (Shows effect of compound interest)			Projected Equity (Shows effect of compound appreciation)		
Initial Draw: $	147,000		Current Property Value: $		500,000
Monthly Draw: $	532.74		Projected Annual Appreciation:		4%
Projected Average Interest Rate:	6.000%		Actuarial Life Expectancy:		14
Mortgage Insurance:	0.500%		Projected Value: $		865,838
Annual Cost:	6.500%		Projected Loan Balance: $		509,686
Actuarial Life Expectancy:	14	years	Projected Equity: $		356,152
Future Balance: $	509,686				

Let's look at this graphically:

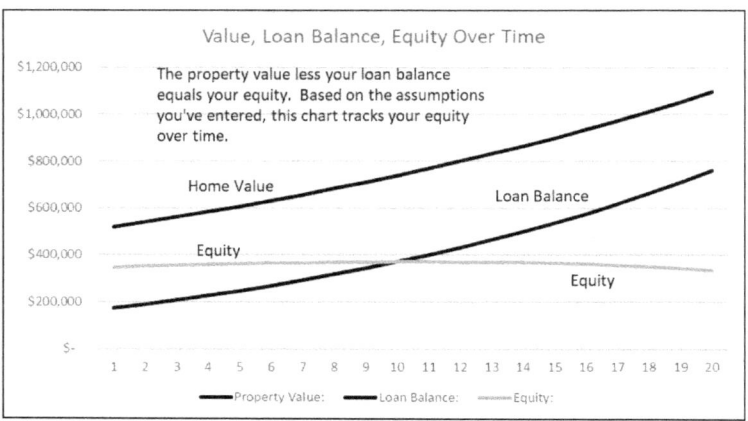

Here you can see that the value of her home grows while the loan balance grows, too. In the meantime, she no longer has to make mortgage payments, and the lender is sending her $532.74 per month.

If Mary lives long enough and if appreciation doesn't exceed our projections, it is possible that one day she would run out of equity. But if Mary is 75 years old today, in 20 years she'll be 95 and still have nearly as much equity as before.

The point is, these loans are quite conservative on purpose. They are designed to last a lifetime, and while there can be no guarantees, they are designed so it's not likely you'll ever owe more than your home is worth. It's possible, yes, even probable if you outlive your expiration date by many years, or if property values crash.

If you do end up owing the lender more than your home is worth, the lender on a HECM will be made whole when HUD purchases the loan, so your heirs will never have to make up a deficiency. Lenders of jumbo loans aren't protected by FHA insurance, but they still cannot come after your heirs for a deficiency judgement. In either case, no one can ask you to leave until and unless you want to.

EQUITY OFTEN DOESN'T SHRINK

Finally, here's an interesting twist to the equity question that most people don't understand. Notice that in the chart above the value of the home and the loan balance are growing at a very similar rate. That doesn't make any sense, does it, since the interest rate is 6 percent and the appreciation is only 4 percent. How does this make any sense at all?

If you remember that the 4 percent appreciation rate applies to the entire value of your home and the 6 percent interest rate applies only to the loan balance, which is usually less than half of the value, it makes sense. In year one, for example, $500,000 of value growing at 4 percent per year would equal appreciation of $20,000.

In contrast, $155,000 of principal balance (your loan amount) growing at 6 percent per year would equal interest accrual of $9,300—less than half of your equity appreciation.

In fact, this is why the equity line in the graph actually *increases* for the first few years, before eventually starting to catch up to the equity growth years later.

CAN YOUR KIDS INHERIT YOUR HOME?

In a word, yes. When you get a reverse mortgage, your home still belongs to you, and you can pass it on to anyone you wish when you die. Your heirs can then pay off the mortgage, either by selling the property, paying it off with cash, refinancing it into a conventional loan, or refinancing it with another reverse mortgage, if they are old enough and qualify.

HOW LONG CAN I LIVE IN OUR HOME IF MY SPOUSE DIES?

Forever. Reverse mortgages are a lifetime loan. As long as one of the borrowers still lives in the home, pays property taxes and insurance and maintains the home, you may keep the home and the mortgage.

CAN THEY TAKE YOUR HOME AND KICK YOU OUT?

Yes. If you don't make property tax payments or maintain the home and keep an insurance policy in place. You must pay all property-related expenses. (Although if you can't, we can set it up so the lender does that for you.)

CHAPTER 11

CASE STUDIES

SINCE EVERY FAMILY has different needs, your needs will be different than the next. The challenge you're trying to solve is not the same as mine. A common myth is that the only people who get reverse mortgages are those who are flat broke and desperate for cash. While a reverse mortgage can often be helpful in that situation, most borrowers are not broke at all.

The various benefits of reverse mortgages can best be illustrated with case studies—actual clients that have taken reverse mortgages and were delighted that they did.

Let's look at the challenges different people faced and how they solved their problems.

NOT ENOUGH MONEY AT THE END OF THE MONTH

ROB — Rob was the kind of client that most people think of when they think of a reverse mortgage candidate. He owned his home of 45 years free and clear. The value of the home was about $2 million. His Social Security income was less than $1,000 a month, and he had no other income, and no real savings. He had to live very conservatively, and even so was usually broke before the end of the month. He sometimes literally went without food.

His doctor's office was in a commercial area with parking meters. If his appointment was at the end of the month, he sometimes didn't have enough change to put in the meters and had to park several blocks away. Did I mention he had severe hip issues?

On occasion he had a small financial emergency, like a car breakdown, and he had no way to take care of it. This was his situation when he came to me.

He could have sold his home, taken the money and moved into a very nice assisted living facility. However, his two adult daughters, who stood to inherit the home, didn't want him to sell because he would have had a capital gains tax bill of about $400,000. Since the house was their entire inheritance, they didn't want to see their inheritance diluted.

We got Rob an HECM equity line with which he fixed his car, did some work on his home, and went out for a steak dinner for the first time in several years.

Rob passed away a couple of years later. He had spent $30,000 getting the mortgage, and another $20,000 in interest cost. The home had appreciated another $200,000 or so. When the daughters sold the home, because the cost basis was stepped up to then-current value, they didn't owe any capital gains taxes at all. They inherited $200,000 more in value and saved $400,000 in taxes. If you do the math, they came out about $550,000 ahead after selling costs. More important, Rob got to live the remainder of his life with dignity and grace in his own home.

NO MORE MORTGAGE PAYMENTS

Sometimes a homeowner just needs to get rid of their mortgage payments. They're doing fine in general, but they are still young and have lots of energy and want to remain active, but don't have enough cash to do what they love to do. Eliminating their mortgage payments allows them to redirect that money to other things that are a lot more fun than paying your mortgage.

ISADORA — Isadora came to me in exactly this situation. She was a young 73-year-old in perfect health who loved to travel and go out with friends.

Her pension and Social Security were enough to pay her living expenses, but she was drawing down her retirement funds each month to help with her mortgage payment. She could continue doing this for quite a while, but she is likely to live for a long time, and to make sure she didn't deplete her entire account she would have to cut back on expenses.

Instead, she chose a lump-sum reverse mortgage to pay off her mortgage and eliminate mortgage payments. She still had to pay property taxes and insurance but she was able to maintain her lifestyle. In fact, she now had a little money left over each month that she could use to take more expensive trips or add to her savings for later in life.

KAREN — Karen was referred to me by her financial advisor. He was concerned her savings would be gone long before Karen wanted to leave her home. Like Isadora, she was in her early 70s but still very healthy and active, and sharp as a tack. She had a home worth about $2 million, on which she owned about $600,000.

Karen's main goal was to generate cash to add to her investment portfolio so it would last longer. I pointed out that, in addition to being able to more than double her portfolio, not having a mortgage payment would make a huge difference in her life. She understood, but shrugged it off; that wasn't her main objective.

We got her a $1 million reverse mortgage, paid off her existing first mortgage, and gave the rest of the cash to her financial advisor to add to her portfolio.

About three months after we closed, she called to tell me what an enormous difference it made not to have mortgage payments. It significantly cut how much money she spent each month, and in fact she and her advisor now figured that she could travel more and still have funds well into her 100s. While it wasn't her main objective, she excitedly told me that not having a mortgage payment changed everything.

For some seniors, just not having to make a mortgage payment makes all the difference.

A FINANCIAL CUSHION IMPROVES QUALITY OF LIFE

Sometimes homeowners just need more cash flow.

MARGE — Marge was referred to me by her financial advisor. She was in her early 80s and had a small Social Security income. In five years, she had drawn her nest egg down from about $200,000 to less than $20,000. She was still healthy and was likely to live for quite a few more years, but literally could not afford to go out to eat with friends or go see a movie. The funds remaining in her nest egg would cover mortgage payments for the next year or so, but no longer.

She thought she would have to sell her home. We talked about a reverse mortgage with monthly payments. By paying off her mortgage with the reverse mortgage we eliminated her biggest expense, her mortgage payment. The lender also sent her another $300 each month. Now she could enjoy her life and use her nest egg for emergencies if they came up.

An interesting thing is that Marge's sons did not want her

to get the reverse mortgage, because they would inherit less money. We had a family meeting, and it was clear that with another $500 of income each month, Marge would be able to make her mortgage payments without drawing down her nest egg, go out to dinner once a week with friends, and see a movie once a week. (She drew up a very detailed budget.)

I suggested that each son contribute $250 a month to their mother so that she could avoid taking the reverse mortgage, avoid depleting what little remained of her emergency funds, and have a little enjoyment in life. They both said they couldn't afford it.

This is common when seniors first consider a reverse mortgage. Often, family members (particularly those who stand to inherit the home) will object. For this reason, I always ask if my clients have anyone in their lives who might have an opinion about whether they should have a reverse mortgage. If so, I recommend we meet with them early in the process to assuage their concerns about how a reverse mortgage works and what the impact on them will be.

FRANK — Sometimes you just need to make sure that you aren't going to run out of money before you run out of lifetime. Frank was a gentleman in his late 70s who had lived conservatively all his life and saved up a nice retirement portfolio. He was very comfortable, had only a small mortgage left with manageable monthly payments, and no other debt. He had no extraordinary expenses that would drain his investments, and he was even able to afford an overseas trip every year or two for vacation.

However, his financial advisor determined he would be out of money within about 10 years. Not terrible, but he also wanted to do more fun things, which would have shortened his financial runway. (He loved sailing, not an inexpensive sport.) He considered a reverse mortgage, but he didn't really need to do anything right away, and he didn't really want to lose his first mortgage, which he had refinanced into a very low interest rate during the previous refinance boom.

We did a lump-sum reverse second mortgage for Frank to add to his portfolio so that he felt more comfortable increasing his spending.

Yes, there is a second mortgage product available now (as of this writing) that can allow you to leave your existing first mortgage in place.

In a couple of years when interest rates decline and he no longer wishes to make a mortgage payment on his first mortgage, we'll consolidate the two loans into one with a traditional reverse mortgage. In the meantime, while the balance on his second mortgage is increasing, he continues to make payments on his first mortgage, paying that balance down.

EMERGENCY RESERVES

ALICE AND DON — Alice and Don were in their mid-70s with a home worth about $700,000. They had paid it off, but then got a small conventional equity line from their bank for emergencies. Don had a stroke, and the medical bills mounted quickly, soon outrunning the equity line. They asked the bank for an increase in their credit limit, but they didn't qualify because they didn't have enough income.

We arranged a line-of-credit HECM for Alice and Don to pay off their conventional equity line and give them enough cash for emergencies, plus a large line of credit to use in the future.

Sadly, Don passed away a couple of years later, but Alice is in good health and still lives in the home where she raised her children. Her children and grandchildren visit her at the "family home" often, and she can live there as long as she wants. This was a few years ago, and the home has now tripled in value from when they got the line of credit, so this has worked out well for the family on many levels.

MANAGE PORTFOLIO

ERIC —— Eric was a successful Silicon Valley engineer with a very nice home worth about $5 million. He had about $1 million in a 401(k), and another $1 million in an investment portfolio. He was very comfortable.

A grandchild asked for help with a $100,000 down payment for his first home. Eric said yes without hesitation—he had the money. But then Eric thought about the fact that he had 12 grandchildren, and realized that there was no way he could help them all out and pay for his own living expenses for the next 20 years.

We arranged a lump-sum jumbo reverse mortgage of about $2 million for Eric. We paid off his existing mortgage and he added the rest to his investment portfolio. He then told all his grandchildren to come to him when they wanted to buy their first house. His reasoning was simple and profound. He wanted to give them the money now, when he could watch them enjoy it, rather than after he was gone.

AVOID CAPITAL GAINS

I won't repeat the story of Rob from above, but just reiterate the point that spending $50,000 on costs and interest on a reverse mortgage over two years saved his daughters $400,000 in capital gains taxes, and they enjoyed two more years of appreciation.

This is often one of the most significant benefits of a reverse mortgage, and the least discussed.

CHAPTER 12

Risks and Downsides

ADJUSTABLE INTEREST RATE

MOST REVERSE MORTGAGES carry an adjustable interest rate. This can be both good and bad. When interest rates are low, your unpaid interest (which, as you remember from previous chapters, is added to your principal balance) grows more slowly. During periods of high interest rates, the unpaid interest accrues more quickly, eating into your equity faster.

LOAN BALANCE GROWS OVER TIME

Because interest accrues on your loan with a reverse mortgage, the amount you owe to the lender increases over time, rather than decreases. The longer you have a reverse mortgage, the more you will owe.

LESA EXPIRES

As we explained in Chapter 3, if you don't have enough income to pay for your property taxes, insurance and regular upkeep, your lender will set up a *Life Expectancy Set-Aside*, or LESA. A portion of the money you are eligible to draw from your reverse mortgage will be set aside to pay for property taxes and insurance on your behalf, much as lenders might do with a conventional mortgage.

However, if you recall from our discussion on how much money you can get, lenders estimate your expiration date. They only set aside enough funds to pay these charges through that date. If you live past that date, either you will need to pay those charges yourself, or you will need to refinance into a new reverse mortgage, with a new LESA.

HIGHER COSTS

The upfront costs and the interest rate of a reverse mortgage are higher than those of a conventional mortgage. That is because the mortgage presents greater risk to the lender.

CHAPTER 13

WHEN TO SAY "NO"
TO A REVERSE MORTGAGE

THERE ARE TIMES when I've counseled clients to not move forward with a reverse mortgage. While I've never seen a situation where a reverse mortgage would not help achieve some of a homeowner's goals, I have met clients for whom it might create as many challenges as it solves. Let's review when that might be the case.

HAZEL

I was referred to Hazel's daughter-in-law by a past client. Hazel was in her early 90s and owned a condominium in a high-cost area. The children were splitting time helping Mom out with daily needs, but they all could see that the time would come—soon—where they would want to hire in-home supportive care. In-home supportive care is VERY expensive, so, they called me to ask about using a reverse mortgage to pay for it.

Their goal was to pull enough money out of the equity to cover their cash needs for a few years. They expressed concern about eating into the equity and wanted to know how much equity they would have left when Mom no longer lived in the home. I asked if they had considered selling the condo and moving Mom into an assisted living facility. They had, but there were two issues: Mom wanted to stay in the home as long as she could, and if they sold before her death there would be a huge capital gains tax bill. There was no significant estate left for the three children besides the home, and Mom wanted to be able to leave them as much equity as she could. The children, naturally, were also in favor of that.

I needed more information, so I had more questions. In-home care is quite expensive, and they would likely eat through the money I could raise from the equity pretty quickly. Plus, caring for Mom had gotten to be quite difficult, and they couldn't pay for 24/7 in-home care; the kids would still have to pitch in.

How likely was it that they would have to move Mom into assisted living anyway before she passed? Quite likely, they thought.

Did Mom have any illness that would make it likely she might not live long? Asked another way, if she did go into assisted living, would she likely need it for a long time? She had no terminal illness, as it turned out, and longevity ran in their family.

I pointed out that if she moved into an assisted living facility and lived for more than a year after leaving her home, that the reverse mortgage would be due. The heirs would either have to pay off the loan in cash, refinance into a conventional mortgage, or sell the home after all.

After digging a little more, we (the family and I) determined that in order to raise enough cash to pay off Mom's reverse mortgage, they would have to refinance their own mortgages to pull cash out of their own homes. If they wanted to refinance their Mom's reverse mortgage they would have to go on title, which might trigger a reassessment of the property, and thus higher property taxes, and might trigger a capital gains event or possibly gift taxes. If they sold the home, it would trigger the capital gains event they wanted to avoid.

This family decided their best option was to hire in-home supportive care, and have each of the children contribute monthly to that cost, until Mom was ready to move into assisted living. At that time, they could rent out her home until she passed. The short-term cost of supporting Mom's needs avoided the costs and risks of a reverse mortgage.

The lesson here is if the heirs face a large capital gains event if the senior can't stay in the home (because they need to move into assisted living,) a reverse mortgage might pose some risk of forcing a capital gains event. This is generally true only in high-cost areas. Through the rest of the country, IRS tax laws might limit the family's exposure to capital gains. (See your accountant.)

BOB AND MARY

Bob and Mary were recent retirees who wanted to travel. Can you use the proceeds from a reverse mortgage for travel? Yes! They wanted to explore Europe, which sounded awesome to me, so I asked them about their plan. The conversation went something like this.

"We're going to rent a villa in Italy for a year and explore from there."

"Wait. A year? What will you do with your home while you're gone?"

"We'll rent it out to help pay for travel expenses."

"Hang on. If you are out of your home for more than 12 months the loan is due and must be paid back."

"Well, we're planning on coming back."

"Sure, but for 12 months it won't be your personal residence. This is one of the requirements to get and keep a reverse mortgage."

"It will still be our personal residence as far as we're concerned."

"Maybe, but not as far as the lender is concerned. For the home to qualify as your personal residence, you must live there for six months and one day of each year."

I recommended that they not do a reverse mortgage. Sure, their plans *might* change, but if not, they would put themselves at risk of being forced to sell their home. They followed my advice and decided renting out the house would have to be enough to finance their travels.

If you have plans that are likely to take you away from home for more than a year (especially if you intend to rent your home out for income) you might be forced to pay off the loan once you have been gone for a year. However, you do not necessarily have to sell the home to pay it off. You can either pay it off in cash or refinance at that time to a conventional loan if you are able.

SARAH

Sarah was a widow for whom I had placed a reverse mortgage several years earlier when interest rates were very low. At the time she elected—against my advice—to take less cash than the lender offered. She felt she wouldn't need all of it and wanted to owe less money when she passed away so her kids would inherit as much as possible.

However, six years later, she wanted more money. The trouble was, interest rates were much higher now. Higher interest rates generally mean a lower initial principal limit. Sarah was older now and her home was worth more, both factors that increased the amount of equity she could access. She still qualified for a little more money, but at the expense of moving all that debt to a much higher interest rate. I produced projections that showed the difference over time, and it was quite a lot.

I had several conversations with her son about the long-term ramifications. To be honest, the son wasn't all that concerned with his inheritance. He was doing fine in life and just wanted his mother to be happy. However, it was important to Sarah to leave as much as possible to her kids. I suggested the kids all pitch in a little money each month to help Sarah survive. Sarah had to agree to live a little more modestly, but it worked out and she will realize her goal of leaving as much equity as possible to her kids.

The lesson here is to take as much money as you are offered by the lender when you get a reverse mortgage. You can always invest the cash you don't need, and you will probably avoid having to come back for more cash at additional fees and possibly a higher interest rate.

TALK TO AN EXPERIENCED, COMPETENT, ETHICAL MORTGAGE ADVISOR

I can't stress this enough. When you call a phone bank because of a TV commercial or a mailer sent to your home, that person is taught how to sell product, not how to counsel seniors. While the risks are generally spelled out in the disclosures that you'll have to sign, the reverse mortgage disclosure package is dozens of pages, sometimes well over 100. Little warnings about the risks involved can be easily buried. You pay nothing extra to work with an expert. This is a resource you want to take advantage of.

CHAPTER 14

ALTERNATIVES TO
A REVERSE MORTGAGE

MANY OF MY CLIENTS go through the entire process of learning about reverse mortgages, see the benefits and understand the risks and costs, and still want to explore all their alternatives before making a commitment.

I get it. Your home is more than an asset. It's your **home**, and watching your equity diminish can be emotionally difficult.

Through conversations with many families, I have concluded that there are six reasonable alternatives to access the equity in your family home. All of them have advantages and disadvantages, just like reverse mortgages, but they are absolutely worth discussing.

CONVENTIONAL LOAN

You can draw money out with a conventional loan. This is usually less expensive than a reverse mortgage and carries a lower interest rate. It's also familiar to us and there is no shortage of mortgage lenders who will fall all over themselves to help you.

However, you must qualify for the new loan, and, of course, you must make payments. If this is a reasonable alternative for you, you should absolutely consider it.

HOME EQUITY LOAN OR LINE OF CREDIT

A Home Equity Line of Credit (HELOC) is an excellent financial management tool and an excellent tool to handle occasional emergencies, such as medical expenses. You can use it to access your equity quickly and easily (often as easily as using a credit card). You can draw on it as you wish, pay it all back when you can, and then use it again. These loans are much less expensive to arrange. In fact, some banks will do them with no fees at all upfront.

Just like a conventional mortgage, you must qualify for this loan. The interest rate is always variable, and the interest rate can usually go as high as 18 percent. You can only draw on the line for 10 years, and then, if you still owe money, you must make payments, typically over the following 15 years, until it is paid in full.

HELOCs can be a good alternative to a reverse mortgage because of the cost savings, but they are more of a short-term solution and solve only a couple of the challenges that a reverse mortgage solves.

SIGNATURE LOAN

Some banks, and some online "fintech" lenders, make signature loans, where they will make a loan based only on your credit-worthiness. The upfront cost of these loans is usually low.

The interest rates are higher than those with HELOCs as a rule, and you still have to qualify with guidelines similar to conventional real estate loans. You have to make payments, of course, and eventually pay back the loan.

SELL YOUR PROPERTY

For many of my clients, selling their home has been a viable option. It immediately frees up their equity—all of it.

Most are reluctant to do so, however, and I understand why. First of all, it's your home. It's more than just an asset. Who wants to sell their home?

Besides that, it's expensive to sell a home, you have to move, and you'll still have to rent or buy another place to live. There may also be capital gains taxes.

There are cases, however, when it makes sense. For instance, if you are ready to downsize or move into a senior living community, letting go of your family home might be the best course of action for you.

GET A ROOMMATE

If you have spare bedrooms, there is nothing wrong with getting a roommate as you get older. I once did a reverse mortgage for four senior ladies who all bought a home together. They were literally the Golden Girls, and not only were they the most delightful clients I've ever had, they all seemed to have a genuinely good time together.

You'll give up your privacy, of course, but the additional rental income, sharing expenses and the companionship might make this one of the best options.

FAMILY SUPPORT

This option is often dismissed much too quickly. I've suggested it many times when potential heirs (typically children) have objected to a reverse mortgage because they would inherit less money if their parents got a reverse mortgage.

I've sat with my clients' children and suggested that Mom would probably be fine with a little extra income each month. If each kid kicked in so much, her cash flow issues would be solved and there would be no need for a reverse mortgage at all.

The children don't always go for it, but in the last three years I've had several families decide it was the best solution for the family in the long run. It's worth considering.

THE BOTTOM LINE

A reverse mortgage is nothing more than a way to use the equity in your home to achieve a goal or meet a challenge.

There are viable alternatives that accomplish the same thing, each with disadvantages and advantages over a reverse mortgage. Do I regret it when a client chooses a different path? Not at all. If my counseling has helped a family make a decision that gives them a better outcome, I've done my job well and I'm happy. And, hopefully, they'll remember me when a friend, family or co-worker mentions they are looking into getting a reverse mortgage.

CONCLUSION

REVERSE MORTGAGES ARE a complex financial product. By now, you can see that they can change your life for the better, but they can cost you dearly if you are not well informed.

The good news is that there is a great deal of good information out there, and most of the products that might work for you are available from numerous sources, at similar terms and costs. No lender can bend the rules for you, and no lender has a magic source of funds. So, when you shop around, the mortgage advisor that you feel most comfortable with has the same products at about the same price and terms as everyone else. So, don't shop for price; shop for an honest mortgage advisor who takes the time to understand your circumstances, goals and concerns, and who communicates clearly and helps you understand the benefits, costs and risks of the type of reverse mortgage you want.

Happy shopping!

ABOUT THE AUTHOR

CASEY FLEMING began his career in the mortgage industry in 1979 as a real estate appraiser. He founded and built one of the largest appraisal and consulting firms in northern California before transitioning to lending in 1995.

Since then, Casey led the development of an award-winning mortgage web site, then founded and ran an online mortgage company. He later built a team of 300 loan officers for a nationwide broker, and published books with the intention of helping consumers make better, well-informed decisions about their mortgage financing. *The Loan Guide: How to Get the Best Possible Mortgage*, was published in 2014. *Buying and Financing Your New Home* was published in 2023. *The Insider's Guide to Reverse Mortgages* is book three of The Loan Guide series.

Casey is a dog lover, having fostered over 30 dogs for rescue organizations, with of course a handful of foster fails. He is also an avid sailor. He has raced Lasers, Hobie Cats, and some big boats, and owns and sails a restored older plastic classic on the San Francisco Bay.

Casey lives in San Carlos with his wife and two cats, and no doubt another couple of dogs in the near future.

Casey has no plans to retire, as he still loves the puzzle of finding the best solution to meet the concerns, goals and circumstances of each client, and loves helping folks figure out how to live a productive and happy retirement.

To learn more about mortgages, visit Casey's web site at LoanGuide.com.

GLOSSARY

Accrues – Grows. In the context of a mortgage, this means that the interest charged on your loan every month is added to the amount you owe, increasing your principal balance, so that the amount you owe *grows*, or becomes larger, every month.

Call – The lender informs you that the loan is due and must be paid in full.

Compound Interest – When interest is charged and added to the loan amount, and then interest is charged again the next month, the interest is said to be *compounding*, meaning that you are now paying interest on the interest.

Conforming Loan Limit – The maximum loan that will be purchased by Fannie Mae or Freddie Mac. This limit changes every year, and in areas with higher-cost real estate may be higher than in areas that are not high cost.

Expected Rate – The average interest rate that the lender expects the loan to carry over the life of the loan. On a fixed-rate reverse mortgage the expected rate is the Note rate, since it's fixed. On an adjustable-rate mortgage the expected rate is set by determining what institutional investors expect interest rate to be over the next 10 years. (For more information, perform an online search for *Swap Rate*.)

Expiration Date – The date a lender believes you will no longer be alive, based on actuarial tables.

FHA – The Federal Housing Agency is the U.S. Agency that insures certain types of mortgages.

Forward Mortgage – A conventional mortgage where you borrow money from your lender, and then make regular installments until the loan is paid back, plus interest.

HECM – Home Equity Conversion Mortgage – a reverse mortgage made by a private lender or bank and insured by FHA

HUD – Housing and Urban Development is a U.S. agency that is the parent agency for FHA.

Index – A measure of interest rate levels in the marketplace, in the same sense that the Dow Jones is a measure of stock prices. The index is used – on adjustable-rate reverse mortgages only – to set your new interest rate upon each adjustment.

Initial Disbursement Limit – The maximum amount that you can borrow in the first year that you have your reverse mortgage.

Initial Principal Limit – the maximum amount you may borrow on a reverse mortgage for a specific loan program, as determined by the Maximum Claim Amount, your age, and the expected interest rate.

Jumbo Reverse Mortgage – Any reverse mortgage that is not insured by FHA mortgage insurance, whether because it is ineligible or because a non-insured product was a better solution for you.

Life Expectancy Set-Aside (or LESA) – An amount set aside from your initial principal limit that is reserved to pay for your property taxes and homeowner's insurance for the duration of your life expectancy.

Line of Credit – A reverse mortgage where the lender advances you funds only when you request them. Best used if you don't need monthly income, but have periodic need for cash for emergencies or periodic expenses.

Lump Sum Reverse Mortgage – In a Lump Sum, or Single Disbursement Lump Sum reverse mortgage you receive one payment, all in one lump sum, at the time of closing. There are no monthly payments after that, and no equity line from which to draw.

Mandatory Charges – These are charges that must be paid when the new reverse mortgage is put in place. They include any liens against your property (e.g. mortgage, home equity line of credit, unpaid property taxes) plus the costs of arranging the reverse mortgage.

Margin – An amount defined in your Note that is added to the index in order to determine your new interest rate each time your rate is adjusted. Applies to adjustable-rate reverse mortgages only.

Maximum Claim Amount – The appraised value or, in the case of a HECM, the conforming loan limit in your area, whichever is lower.

Monthly Tenure Reverse Mortgage – A reverse mortgage where you receive monthly payments for the rest of your life.

Monthly Term Reverse Mortgage – Same as a monthly tenure, but the monthly payments are set for a defined term (number of years.) This is a good option if you want to receive large monthly payments and don't need them for an indefinite period of time, but rather for a specified number of years.

Non-borrowing spouse – A spouse who is on title, but who will not be on the loan. There may be several reasons for this. The most common is that the non-borrowing spouse is not yet old enough to qualify for the reverse mortgage.

NOTE – The agreement between you and the lender whereby the lender agrees to lend you money at specific terms, and you agree to pay it back as proscribed by the Note.

Origination Fee – A fee charged by your lender or broker to arrange your loan.

Principal Limit Factor – A factor applied to the maximum claim amount to determine your Initial Principal Limit (or how much you can borrow.)

Term – How long will a mortgage last. The term of a conventional mortgage is how long you have until you must pay it all back. A reverse mortgage is an open term, meaning that the length of time you will have the loan is not defined, but rather dependent on other factors, such as how long you will live and whether or not you continue to live in your home.

Underwater – This describes the situation where the amount you owe on your loan exceeds the current value of the home.

Unpaid Principal Balance – The current balance of what you owe at any given point in time.

Endnotes

1   "Some Say the U.S. Is on the Brink of a Retirement Crisis.
     See Whether You Agree -- and What You Want to Do
     About It," 1 February 2025, Some Say the U.S. Is on the
     Brink of a Retirement Crisis. See Whether You Agree --
     and What You Want to Do About It. | The Motley Fool,
     (Accessed 31 March, 2025)

2   "Fact Sheet: Aging in the United States," 13 January,
     2016, https://www.prb.org/aging-unitedstates-fact-sheet/,
     (Accessed 12 November, 2018).

3   "Why Older Workers Can't Get Hired," 18 May, 2012,
     https://money.usnews.com/money/blogs/planning-to-re-
     tire/2012/05/18/why-older-workers-cant-get-hired,
     (Accessed 12 November, 2018)

4   "Homeowners Are Sitting on $34.7 Trillion in Equity—
     but Mortgage Debt Is Growing" 31 March, 2025
     Homeowners Are Sitting on $34.7 Trillion in Equity
     Despite Growing Debt, (Accessed 31 March, 2025

5   "Bankruptcy Soars Among Elders as Inequality Deepens,"
     Andrew Soergel, 8 August 2018, https://money.usnews.
     com/money/blogs/planning-to-retire/2012/05/18/why-old-
     er-workers-cant-get-hired, (Accessed 13 November, 2018)

6   If you choose the lump-sum, fixed-rate HECM, the amount of your equity that you can access may be limited to less than the initial principal balance. See discussion on Lump Sum HECMs.

7   For those reading a paper-based book, the web site to look up conforming loan limits is: https://www.fanniemae.com/singlefamily/loan-limits

8   "What is the Cost of In-Home Care?" 12 June 2024, Average Cost of In-Home Care 2025: Per Month & Per Hour | ConsumerAffairs® (Accessed 31 March, 2025)

www.ingramcontent.com/pod-product-compliance
Lightning Source LLC
Chambersburg PA
CBHW070630130626

46555CB00006B/2507